Important Instru

Students, Parents, and Teachers can use the URL or QR code provided below to access Lumos back to school refresher online assessment. Please note that this assessment is provided in the Online format only.

URL
Visit the URL below and place the book access code **http://www.lumoslearning.com/a/tedbooks** **Access Code: BS56L-47321-P**
OR **Scan the QR code with your Smartphone** 

Lumos Back-to-School Refresher tedBook - 6th Grade English Language Arts, Back to School book to address Summer Slide designed for classroom and home use

Contributing Author	-	Julie Turner
Contributing Author	-	Brenda Green
Contributing Author	-	George Smith
Contributing Author	-	Wendy Bundgaard
Executive Producer	-	Mukunda Krishnaswamy
Designer and Illustrator	-	Devraj Dharmaraj

COPYRIGHT ©2019 by Lumos Information Services, LLC. **ALL RIGHTS RESERVED.** No part of this work covered by the copyright hereon may be reproduced or used in any form or by an means graphic, electronic, or mechanical, including photocopying, recording, taping, Web distribution or information storage and retrieval systems- without the written permission of the publisher.

NGA Center/CCSSO are the sole owners and developers of the Common Core State Standards, which does not sponsor or endorse this product. © Copyright 2010. National Governors Association Center for Best Practices and Council of Chief State School Officers.

ISBN-13: 978-1-081938-13-0

Printed in the United States of America

For permissions and additional information contact us

Lumos Information Services, LLC
PO Box 1575, Piscataway, NJ 08855-1575
http://www.LumosLearning.com

Email: support@lumoslearning.com
Tel: (732) 384-0146
Fax: (866) 283-6471

Developed by Expert Teachers

Table of Contents

Online Program Benefits	I
Introduction	1

Chapter 1 Reading: Literature — 3

RL.5.1	Supporting Statements	4
RL.5.1	Drawing Inferences	6
RL.5.2	Theme	10
RL.5.2	Characters	13
RL.5.2	Summarizing Texts	15
RL.5.3	Events	18
RL.5.3	Setting	20
RL.5.4	Figurative Language	24
RL.5.5	Structures of Text	25
RL.5.6	Styles of Narration	26
RL.5.7	Visual Elements	27
RL.5.9	Compare and Contrast	29
	Answer Key & Detailed Explanations	30

Chapter 2 Reading: Informational Text — 38

RI.5.1	Inferences and Conclusions	39
RI.5.2	Main Idea and Supporting Details	40
RI.5.3	Text Relationships	42
RI.5.4	General Academic Vocabulary	45
RI.5.5	Text Structure	46
RI.5.6	Point of View	47
RI.5.7	Locating Answers	48
RI.5.8	Using Evidence to Support Claims	49
RI.5.9	Integrating Information	50
	Answer Key & Detailed Explanations	52

Chapter 3	**Language**	58
L.5.1.A	Prepositional Phrases	59
L.5.1.B	Verbs	60
L.5.1.C	Subject-Verb Agreement	61
L.5.1.D	Adjectives and Adverbs	62
L.5.1.E	Correlative Conjunctions	63
L.5.2.A	Capitalization	64
L.5.2.A	Punctuation	65
L.5.2.B	Commas in Introductory Phrases	66
L.5.2.C	Using Commas	67
L.5.2.D	Writing Titles	68
L.5.2.E	Spelling	69
L.5.3.A	Sentence Structure	70
L.5.3.B	Varieties of English	71
L.5.4.A	Context Clues	72
L.5.4.B	Roots and Affixes	73
L.5.4.C	Reference Sources	74
L.5.5.A	Interpreting Figurative Language	75
L.5.5.B	Idioms, Adages, and Proverbs	76
L.5.5.C	Synonyms and Antonyms	77
L.5.6	Vocabulary	78
	Answer Key & Detailed Explanations	79

Additional Information	90

INTRODUCTION

This book is specifically designed to help diagnose and remedy Summer Learning Loss in students that are starting their sixth grade classes. It provides a comprehensive and efficient review of 5th Grade English Language Arts standards through an online assessment. Before starting sixth grade instruction, parents/teachers can administer this online test to their students. After the students complete the test, a standards mastery report is immediately generated to pinpoint any proficiency gaps. Using the diagnostic report and the accompanying study plan, students can get targeted remedial practice through lessons included in this book to overcome any Summer learning loss.

Addressing the Summer slide during the first few weeks of a new academic will help students have a productive sixth grade experience.

The online program also gives your student an opportunity to briefly explore various standards that are included in the 6th grade curriculum.

Some facts about Summer Learning Loss
- Students often lose an average of 2 and ½ months of math skills
- Students often lose 2 months of reading skills
- Teachers spend at least the first 4 to 5 weeks of the new school year reteaching important skills and concepts

Lumos Learning Back-To-School Refresher Methodology
The following graphic shows the key components of the Lumos back-to-school refresher program.

5th Grade Online Diagnostic Test → **Record Summer Learning Loss** → **Remediate Summer Learning loss** → **Ready For Grade 6**

© Lumos Information Services 2019 | LumosLearning.com

Name: _____   Date: _____

Chapter 1
How to Use this Book Effectively

Step 1: Access Online Diagnostic Assessment

Use the URL and access code provided below or scan the QR code to access the Diagnostic assessment and get started. The online diagnostic test helps to measure the summer loss and remediate loss in an efficient and effective way.

After completing the test, your student will receive immediate feedback with detailed reports on standards mastery. With this report, use the next section of the book to design a practice plan for your student to overcome the summer loss.

URL	QR Code
Visit the URL below and place the book access code http://www.lumoslearning.com/a/tedbooks **Access Code: BS56L-47321-P**	

Name: _____   Date: _____

Step 2: Review the Personalized Study Plan Online

After you complete the online practice test, access your individualized study plan from the table of contents (Figure 1)

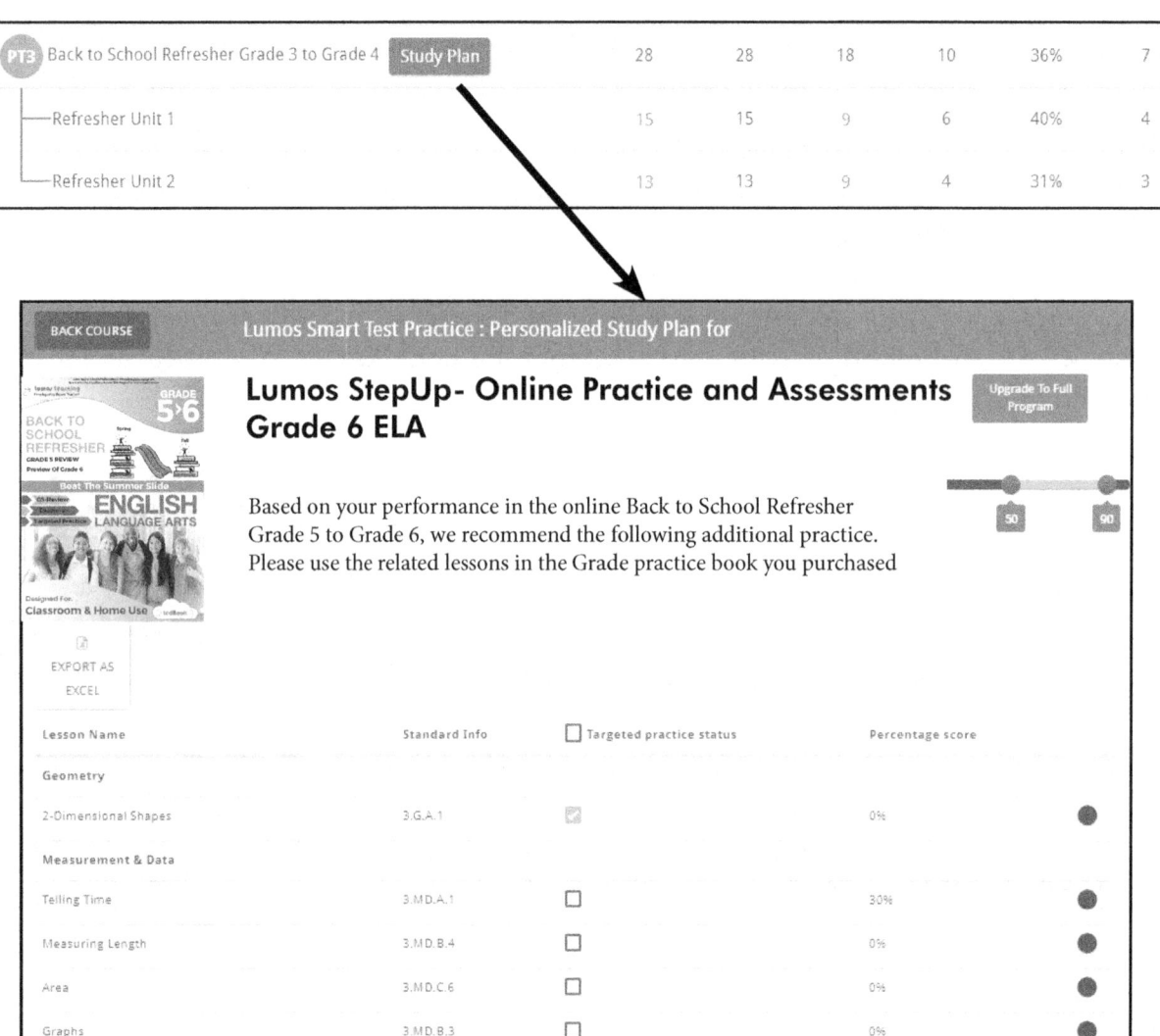

Step 3: Remediate Summer Learning Loss

Using the information provided in the study plan report, complete the targeted practice using the appropriate lessons in this book to overcome Summer learning loss. Using the Lesson Name, find the appropriate practice lessons in this book and answer the questions provided. After completing the practice in the book you can mark the progress in your study plan as shown the figure 1. Please use the answer key and detailed answers provided for each lesson to gain further understanding of the learning objective.

© Lumos Information Services 2019 | LumosLearning.com

Reading: Literature

RL.5.1 Supporting Statements
The Glass Cupboard

There was a king who had a cupboard that was made entirely of glass. It was a special cupboard. It looked empty, but you could always take out anything you wanted. There was only one thing that had to be remembered. Whenever something was taken out of it, something else had to be put back in, although nobody knew why.

One day some thieves broke into the palace and stole the cupboard. "Now, we can have anything we want," they said. One of the thieves said, "I want a large bag of gold," and he opened the glass cupboard and got it. The other two did the same and they, too, got exactly what they wanted. The thieves forgot one thing. Not one of them put anything back inside the cupboard.

This went on and on for weeks and months. At last, the leader of the thieves could bear it no longer. He took a hammer and smashed the glass cupboard into a million pieces, and then all three thieves fell down dead.

When the king returned home, he ordered his servants to search for the cupboard. When the servants found it and the dead thieves, they filled sixty great carts with the gold and took it back to the king. He said, "If those thieves had only put something back into the cupboard, they would be alive to this day."

He ordered his servants to collect all of the pieces of glass and melt into a globe of the world with all the countries on it, this was to remind himself and others, to give back something in return when someone shows an act of kindness or gives us something.

After reading the story, enter the details in the map below. This will help you to answer the questions with ease.

Name: _____   Date: _____

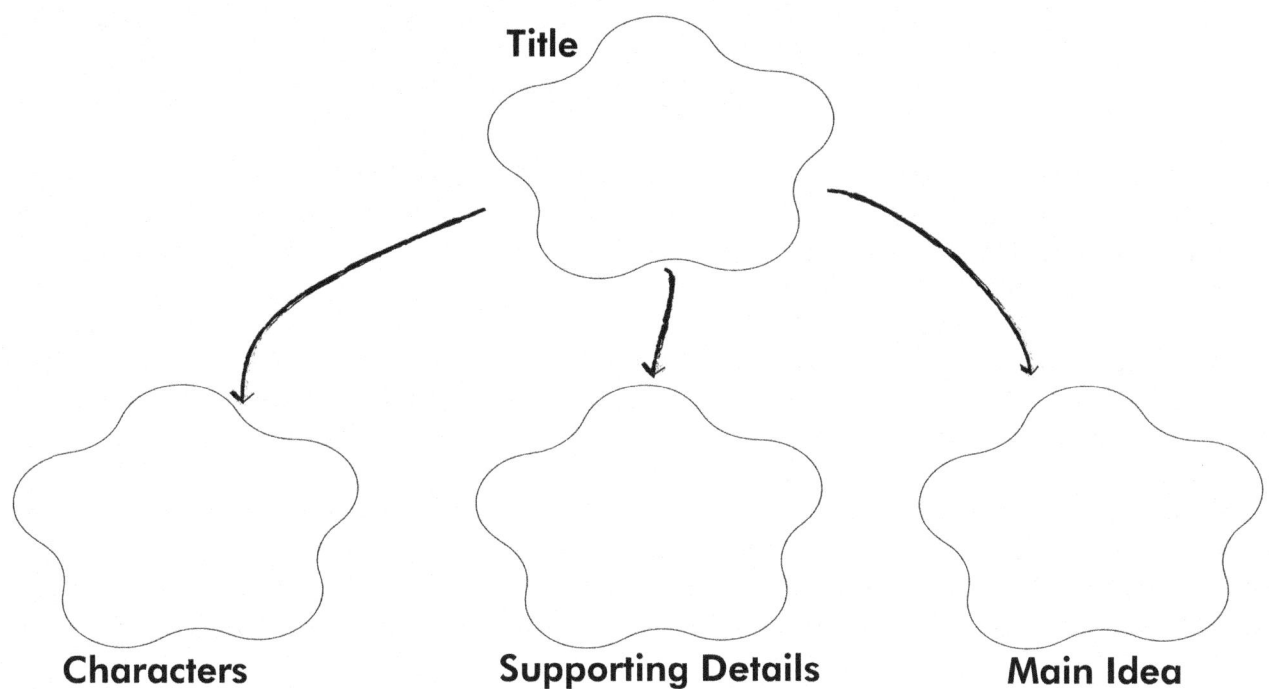

1. What happened when the king was away?

Ⓐ There was a storm, and it smashed the glass cupboard.
Ⓑ The people in the palace accidentally broke the glass cupboard.
Ⓒ Some thieves broke into the palace and stole the glass cupboard.
Ⓓ None of the above

2. What did the thieves take out of the cupboard?

Ⓐ They took out bags of gold.
Ⓑ They took out bags of silver.
Ⓒ They took out bags of diamonds.
Ⓓ They took out bags of stones.

3. What did the thieves forget to do?

Ⓐ They forgot to take out everything that was in the cupboard every time.
Ⓑ They forgot to break the cupboard each time they took something out.
Ⓒ They forgot to take out the jewels.
Ⓓ They forgot to put something back each time they took something out.

RL.5.1 Drawing Inferences

The Traveler

A weary traveler stopped at Sam's house and asked him for shelter for the night. Sam was a friendly soul. He not only agreed to let the traveler stay for the night, and he decided to treat his guest to some curried chicken. So he bought a couple of chickens from the market and gave them to his wife to cook. Then, he went off to buy some fruit.

Now, Sam's wife could not resist food. She had a habit of eating as she cooked. So as she cooked the meat, she smelled the rich steam and could not help tasting a piece. It was tender and delicious, and she decided to have another piece. Soon, there was only a tiny bit left.

Her little son, Kevin, ran into the kitchen. She gave him that little piece. Kevin found it so tasty that he begged his mother for more. But, there was no more chicken left. The traveler, who had gone to have a wash, returned. The woman heard him coming and had to think of a plan quickly. She began to scold her son loudly: "Your father has taught you a shameful and disgusting habit. Stop it, I tell you!"

The traveler was curious. "What habit has his father taught the child?" he asked.

"Oh," said the woman, "Whenever a guest arrives, my husband cuts off their ears and roasts them for my son to eat."

The traveler was shocked. He picked up his shoes and fled. "Why has our guest left in such a hurry?" asked Sam when he came back.

"A fine guest indeed!" exclaimed his wife. "He snatched the chickens out of my pot and ran off with them!"

"The chickens!" exclaimed Sam. He ran after his guest, shouting, "Let me have one, at least; you may keep the other!" But, his guest only ran faster!

After reading the story, enter the details in the map below. This will help you to answer the questions with ease.

Name: _____   Date: _____

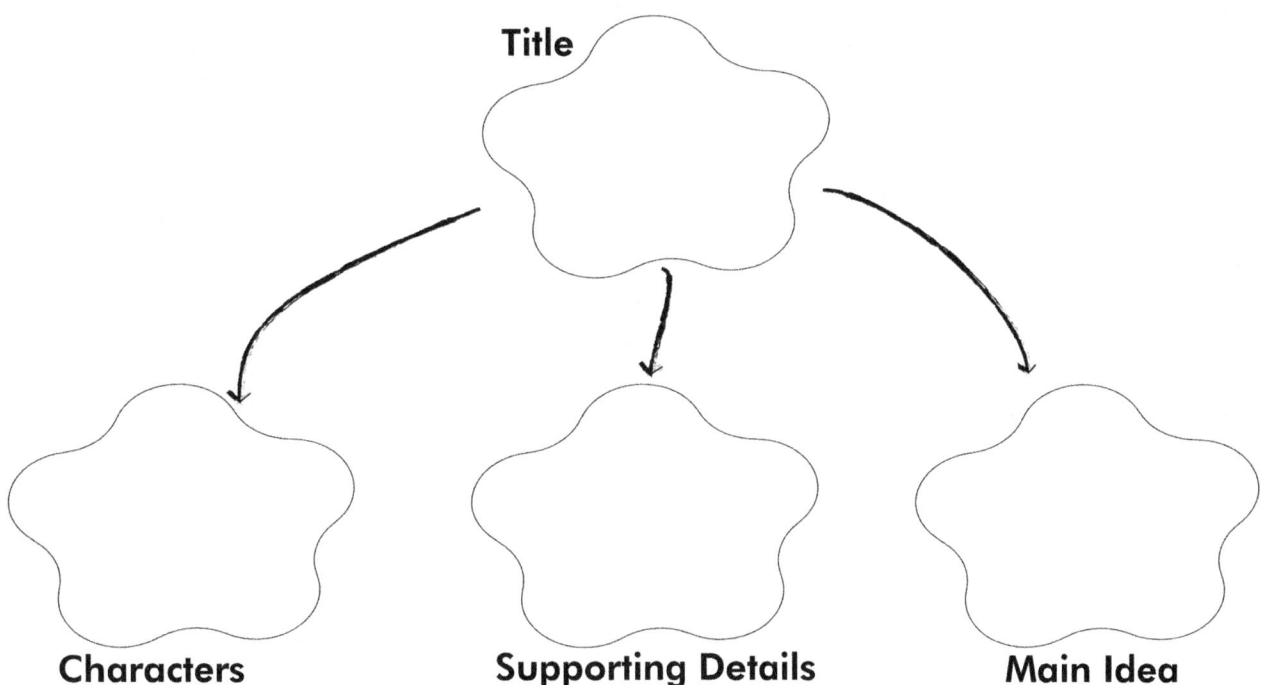

1. According to the above story, what kind of a man was Sam?

    Ⓐ He was a friendly and helpful man.
    Ⓑ He was a dangerous and cruel man.
    Ⓒ He was a miserly and cunning man.
    Ⓓ He was a friendly and miserable man.

2. According to the above story, how can you describe the character of Sam's wife?

    Ⓐ She liked food a lot.
    Ⓑ She was very cunning and clever.
    Ⓒ She was a very good cook.
    Ⓓ All of the above

Do Your Best

Katie stood before the crowd blushing and wringing her hands. She looked out and saw the room full of faces. Some she knew, and some she did not. But, they were all here to listen to her. Taking a deep breath, she opened her mouth, but no words came out. Tears formed in the corners of her eyes as she closed them.

With her eyes closed, she imagined her mother helping her get dressed and ready for tonight. "Just do your best," is what her mother had told her.

She opened her eyes and found her mother's smiling face in the crowd. Relaxing, she took another deep breath and started singing. She did not stop until she finished, and the crowd was on their feet applauding.

After the show, she found her parents and her friends. They all had wonderful things to say about her song and how proud they were because she kept going even when it seemed like she might give up. She shrugged her shoulders and shared a smile with her mother.

"I just did my best," she answered.

After reading the story, enter the details in the map below. This will help you to answer the questions with ease.

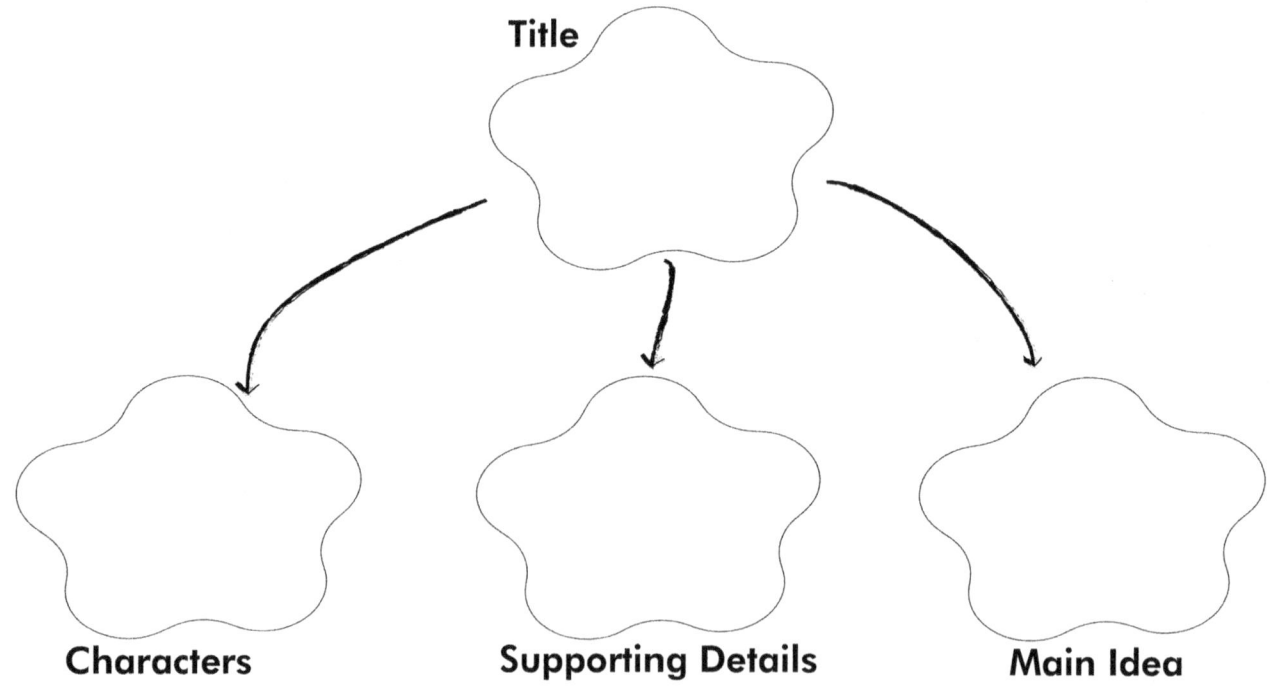

Name: _____   Date: _____

3. The above passage is about _____.

  Ⓐ being determined
  Ⓑ giving up
  Ⓒ listening to friends
  Ⓓ taking a deep breath

4. At the beginning of the story, how was Katie feeling?

  Ⓐ Katie was friendly.
  Ⓑ Katie was excited.
  Ⓒ Katie was depressed.
  Ⓓ Katie was nervous.

Name: _____   Date: _____

RL.5.2 Theme

The Glass Cupboard

There was a king who had a cupboard that was made entirely of glass. It was a special cupboard. It looked empty, but you could always take out anything you wanted. There was only one thing that had to be remembered. Whenever something was taken out of it, something else had to be put back in, although nobody knew why.

One day some thieves broke into the palace and stole the cupboard. "Now, we can have anything we want," they said. One of the thieves said, "I want a large bag of gold," and he opened the glass cupboard and got it. The other two did the same and they, too, got exactly what they wanted. The thieves forgot one thing. Not one of them put anything back inside the cupboard.

This went on and on for weeks and months. At last, the leader of the thieves could bear it no longer. He took a hammer and smashed the glass cupboard into a million pieces, and then all three thieves fell down dead.

When the king returned home, he ordered his servants to search for the cupboard. When the servants found it and the dead thieves, they filled sixty great carts with the gold and took it back to the king. He said, "If those thieves had only put something back into the cupboard, they would be alive to this day."

He ordered his servants to collect all of the pieces of glass and melt into a globe of the world with all the countries on it, this was to remind himself and others, to give back something in return when someone shows an act of kindness or gives us something.

After reading the story, enter the details in the map below. This will help you to answer the question with ease.

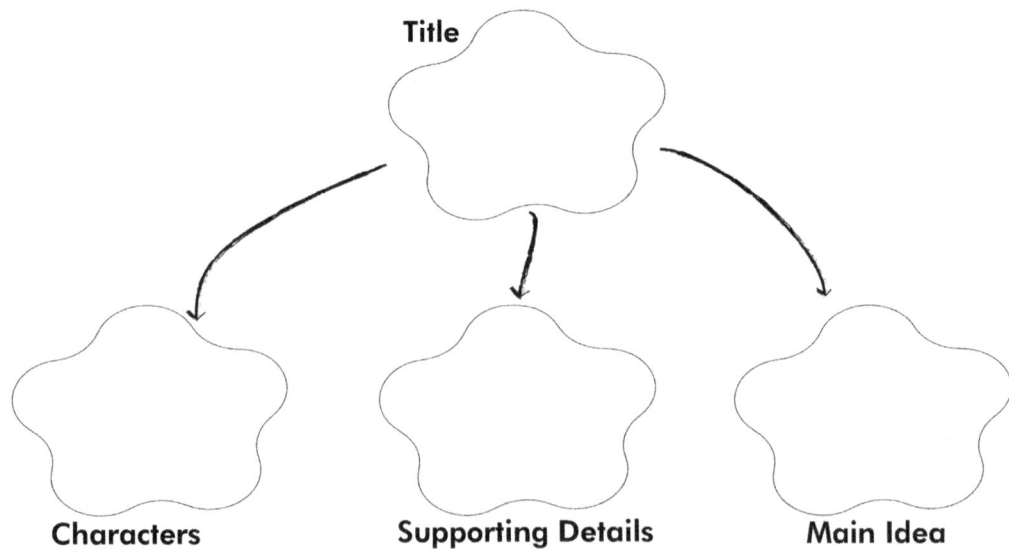

Name: _____   Date: _____

1. What is the purpose of this story?

Ⓐ This story is about learning how to break a glass cupboard.
Ⓑ This story is about learning the importance of gold.
Ⓒ This story is about giving something back in return.
Ⓓ This story is about a king.

What is this life if, full of care,
We have no time to stand and stare?

No time to stand beneath the boughs
And stare as long as sheep or cows.

No time to see, when woods we pass,
Where squirrels hide their nuts in grass

No time to see, in broad daylight,
Streams full of stars, like skies at night.

No time to turn at Beauty's glance,
And watch her feet, how they can dance.

No time to wait till her mouth can
Enrich that smile her eyes began.

A poor life if, full of care,
We have no time to stand and stare.

- W. H. Davies

2. What is the poet saying in the last stanza of the poem?

Ⓐ This stanza is saying that life is poor even if you have everything, because you have no time to stand and stare.
Ⓑ This stanza is saying that life is not good.
Ⓒ This stanza is saying that there is no time to stand and stare, so life is good.
Ⓓ None of the above

Name: _____   Date: _____

3. Choose a suitable title for this poem.

Ⓐ Life
Ⓑ Stare
Ⓒ Stop and Stare
Ⓓ Life and Stare

Name: _____   Date: _____

RL.5.2 Characters

Do Your Best

Katie stood before the crowd blushing and wringing her hands. She looked out and saw the room full of faces. Some she knew and some she did not. But, they were all here to listen to her. Taking a deep breath, she opened her mouth but no words came out. Tears formed in the corners of her eyes as she closed them.

With her eyes closed, she imagined her mother helping her get dressed and ready for tonight. "Just do your best," is what her mother had told her. She opened her eyes and found her mother's smiling face in the crowd. Relaxing, she took another deep breath and started singing. She did not stop until she finished and the crowd was on their feet applauding.

After the show, she found her parents and her friends. They all had wonderful things to say about her song and how proud they were because she kept going even when it seemed like she might give up. She shrugged her shoulders and shared a smile with her mother. "I just did my best," she answered.

After reading the story, enter the details in the map below. This will help you to answer the questions with ease.

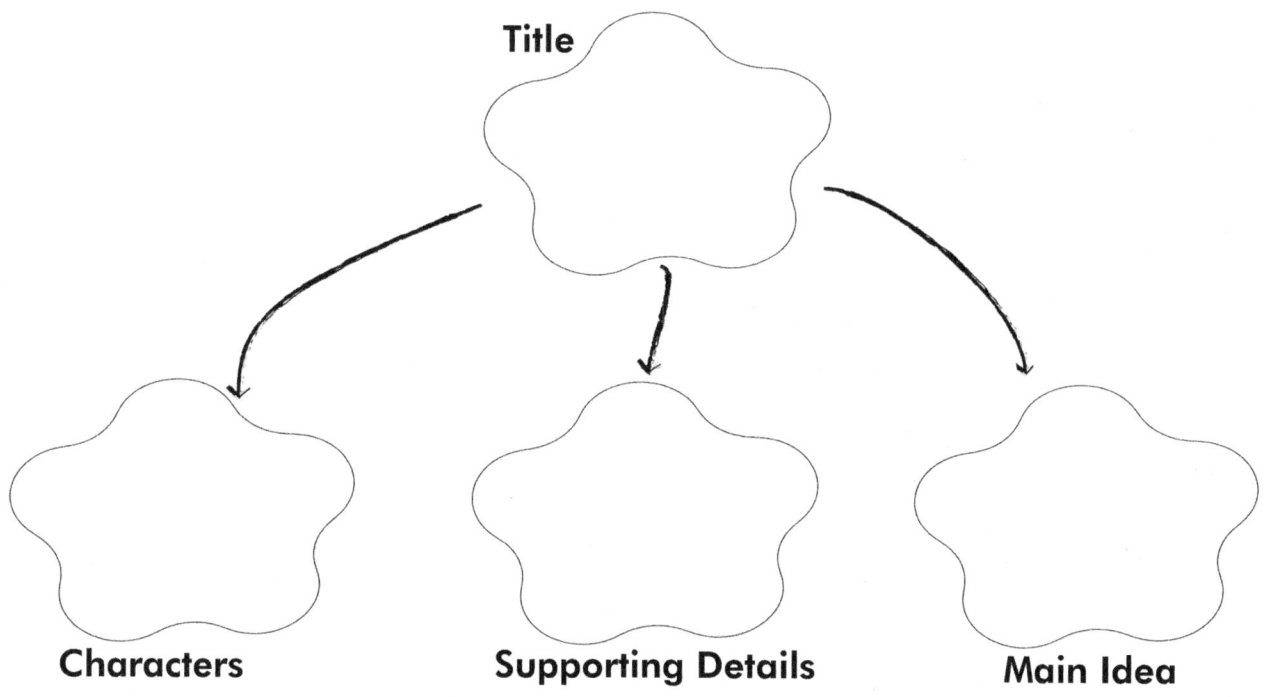

1. **Who are the main characters in the above story?**

    Ⓐ Katie, her mother, and her friends
    Ⓑ Katie and her mother
    Ⓒ Katie and her parents
    Ⓓ Katie and her friends

2. **Who are the secondary characters is this story?**

    Ⓐ Katie and her mother
    Ⓑ Katie's father and her mother
    Ⓒ Katie's father and her friends
    Ⓓ Katie and her friends

3. **What does this story say about Katie's mother?**

    Ⓐ She was very supportive.
    Ⓑ She was not supportive.
    Ⓒ She did not believe in singing.
    Ⓓ She wanted her daughter to make friends.

RL.5.2 Summarizing Texts

What is this life if, full of care,
We have no time to stand and stare?

No time to stand beneath the boughs
And stare as long as sheep or cows.

No time to see, when woods we pass,
Where squirrels hide their nuts in grass

No time to see, in broad daylight,
Streams full of stars, like skies at night.

No time to turn at Beauty's glance,
And watch her feet, how they can dance.

No time to wait till her mouth can
Enrich that smile her eyes began.

A poor life if, full of care,
We have no time to stand and stare.

- W. H. Davies

1. What is the above poem about?

Ⓐ It is about life.
Ⓑ It is about how busy our lives are occasionally.
Ⓒ It is about the importance of taking time to do things that you like.
Ⓓ It is about life not being fair.

Try Again

Surfing is one of Daniel's favorite pastimes! Every weekend when he has the time, he heads toward Port Aransas, Texas with his father. Daniel's family doesn't live far away, so it takes them only about 30 minutes to get there, if there is a short ferry line. They always make sure to get their things ready the night before. Daniel and his dad like to get an early start to their surfing day!

The night before, Daniel makes sure that his dad's truck is clean, especially the bed of the truck where he puts his surfboards. He also takes time to clean his wetsuit that he wears for protection and warmth. His mom usually makes sandwiches, and snacks ahead of time and puts them in the refrigerator to keep them fresh.

Daniel and his dad leave around 5:30 or 6:00 am when the sun is just coming up. Daniel has been surfing with his dad since he was very small. He remembers when his dad would ride with him on the surfboard.

When Daniel was about 9 years old, he fell off of a surfboard and hurt his leg and back. His dad rushed him to a nearby hospital for X-rays and a checkup. Luckily, there were no broken bones. However, the incident claimed Daniel so much that he refused to go surfing for several months. His dad kept encouraging him to give it a try. He told him, "If at once you don't succeed, try, and try again!" Daniel didn't want to try again. He was afraid of getting hurt and falling off of the surfboard.

Finally, Daniel went surfing with his father again. His father went out into the waves, and rode a wave in. Daniel went out on the waves, too. He stayed out for a long time without attempting to ride a wave back to shore. Daniel's dad began to wonder if his son had given up.

Just then a large wave began building up far out in the water. Daniel's dad was astonished! There was Daniel riding the huge wave all the way to shore without a problem. His dad motioned for Daniel to come where he was, but Daniel didn't. Instead he went right back into the water, and began riding wave after wave after wave!

It is amazing that fear can be overcome with one's personal best.

Name: _____   Date: _____

After reading the story, enter the details in the map below. This will help you to answer the questions with ease.

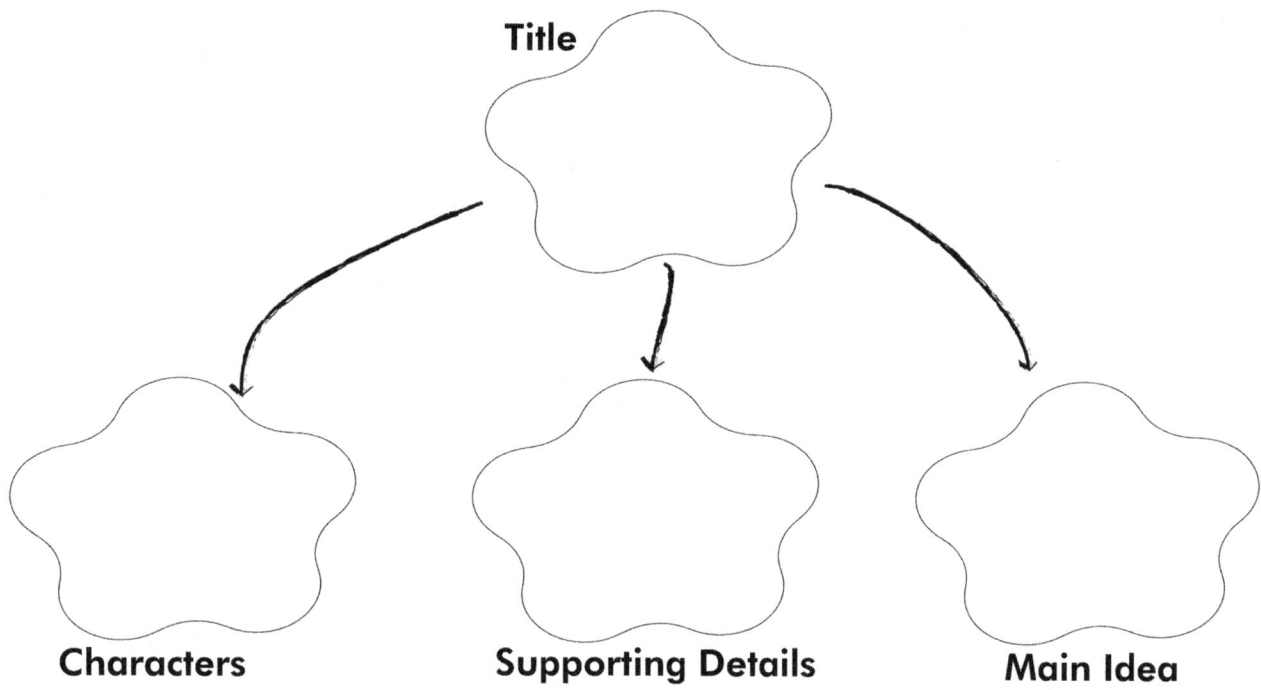

2. What is the story about?

   Ⓐ Never give up when you have a surfboard.
   Ⓑ Keep trying and you will do your best.
   Ⓒ Listen to the waves.
   Ⓓ Give up if you don't want to do something.

3. What does the first paragraph tell the reader?

   Ⓐ Daniel doesn't like to go surfing with his dad.
   Ⓑ Daniel and his dad enjoy going surfing together.
   Ⓒ Daniel got hurt one time surfing.
   Ⓓ Daniel gives up easily.

4. The second paragraph tells how Daniel _____.

   Ⓐ is never ready on time to go surfing.
   Ⓑ doesn't like to get his things ready the night before they go surfing
   Ⓒ gets his things ready early the night before to go surfing
   Ⓓ always forgets something when they go surfing.

Name: _____   Date: _____

RL.5.3 Events

Morning Ride

As the sun was gradually rising across the plain, Chloe was preparing to saddle up her favorite horse, Pepper, to go for a morning ride. First she had to be sure the blanket was in place before getting the saddle. Chloe didn't mind the heavy weight of the saddle as she took it down from the rack and quickly threw it over Pepper's back. Sometimes she did wonder why the weight never bothered horses. Tightening the girth under the saddle would be the hardest part of all. If it was not just right, the saddle could slip causing a problem and possible injury to Chloe while riding. Finally, it was snug and secure.

Of course, Chloe took off the halter so that she could put on the bit and bridle along with the reins. Horses will follow people easier to the barn if they have on a halter. Chloe knew that Pepper would be no problem with her as Chloe kept her tack clean. The condition of the tack was so important in horse care.

Chloe's grandfather, Morgan, had always taught her to take pride in her care of horses. He told her many a time that the horse weighed over twelve hundred pounds. She needed to be sure to respect that and keep it in mind, but not to fear the horse.

She had been raised with horses since she was about two years old. She was taught to ride with someone leading her around. Chloe did not ride with saddles when she was little, just bareback. Saddling up came when Chloe was old enough to handle both saddle and tack.

Leading Pepper out of the barn was easy, as Chloe knew she was anxious for a morning run, as well.

One gentle but firm nudge on Pepper's sides and off they went as fast as lightning. The cool breeze blew through Chloe's hair and Pepper's mane. This was the way to start a new day!

After reading the story, enter the details in the map below. This will help you to answer the questions with ease.

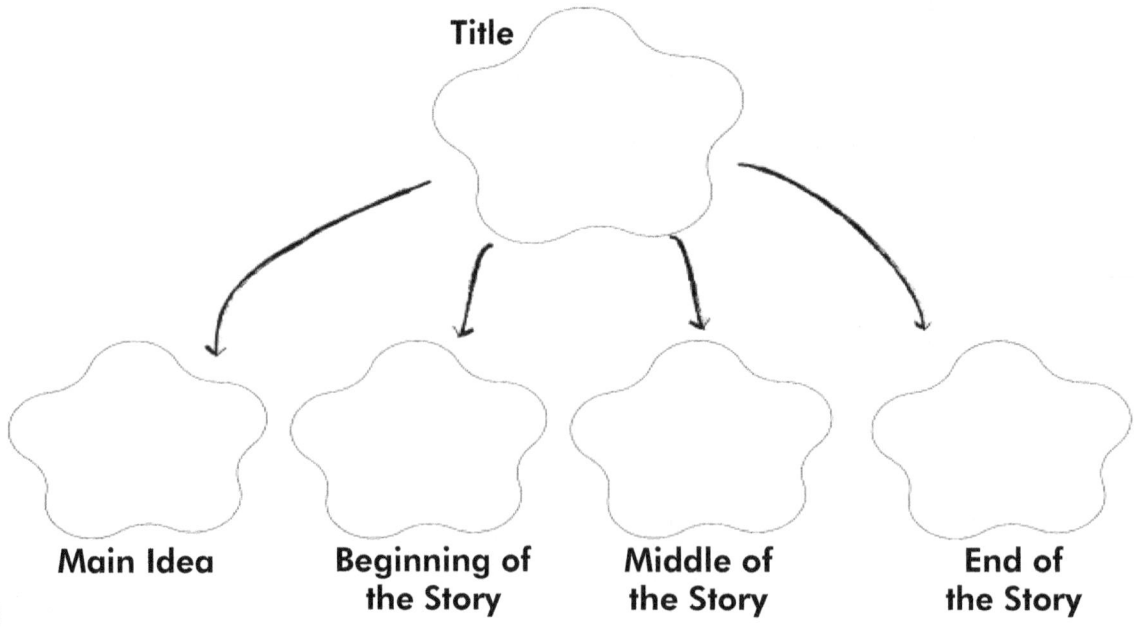

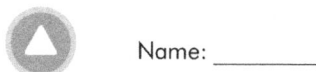

Name: _____ Date: _____

1. **What is the first thing that Chloe does when getting ready to ride Pepper?**

    Ⓐ Chloe puts the saddle on.
    Ⓑ Chloe tightens the girth underneath the horse.
    Ⓒ Chloe puts the saddle blanket on.
    Ⓓ The sun is shining brightly.

2. **Which is the correct order of events?**

    Ⓐ Chloe puts the saddle blanket on. She then tightens the girth. She carefully places the saddle on Pepper. She takes off the halter and puts on the bit and bridle.
    Ⓑ Chloe takes the saddle down and throws it over Pepper. She puts the blanket on Pep per. She tightens the girth. She gallops away.
    Ⓒ Chloe takes the saddle down and throws it across Pepper's backside. She tightens the girth. She puts the blanket on Pepper. She rides away.
    Ⓓ Chloe puts the saddle blanket on Pepper. Then she takes down the saddle and quickly throws it on Pepper's back. She tightens the girth securely. She puts on the bit and bridle after taking off the halter.

3. **Using the letter at the beginning of each sentence, put the sentences into the correct order to make a paragraph.**

A. Emily asks her mother to put the pan in the oven.
B. Emily loves to cook.
C. Emily loves brownies.
D. Emily asks her mother if she can make a snack.
E. She mixes the brownie mix, eggs, and oil together and pours them in a pan.

    Ⓐ B, C, D, E, A
    Ⓑ B, D, C, E, A
    Ⓒ A, B, D, E, C
    Ⓓ E, C, A, D, B

RL.5.3 Setting

Late for School

Marrah heard the brakes on the bus as she shoveled the rest of her breakfast into her mouth. "You just missed the bus!" Marrah's mother yelled. "Why can't you ever be on time?"

"I'm sorry, Mom," Marrah sighed. She ran upstairs to her room so she could get her backpack, knowing she needed to hurry because her mother would have to take her to school.

"Let's go, Marrah!" Her mother called from downstairs. "You don't want to be late for school too!"

Frantic now, Marrah lifted her sheets to look under them before dropping to her knees in front of her bed. She pushed mounds of clothes out of the way as she continued to search for her backpack.

"Marrah!" Her mother called again. She could hear the impatience in her mother's voice downstairs. She ran out of her room and leaned over the rail.

"I can't find my backpack!" She cried out.

"You mean this one?" Her mother pulled the bag from the floor beside her.

"Oh," she replied, her shoulders sagging as she walked down the stairs.

"Let's go to school, Marrah." Her mother said with a small smile on her face as they walked out the door.

Name: _____   Date: _____

After reading the story, enter the details in the map below. This will help you to answer the question with ease.

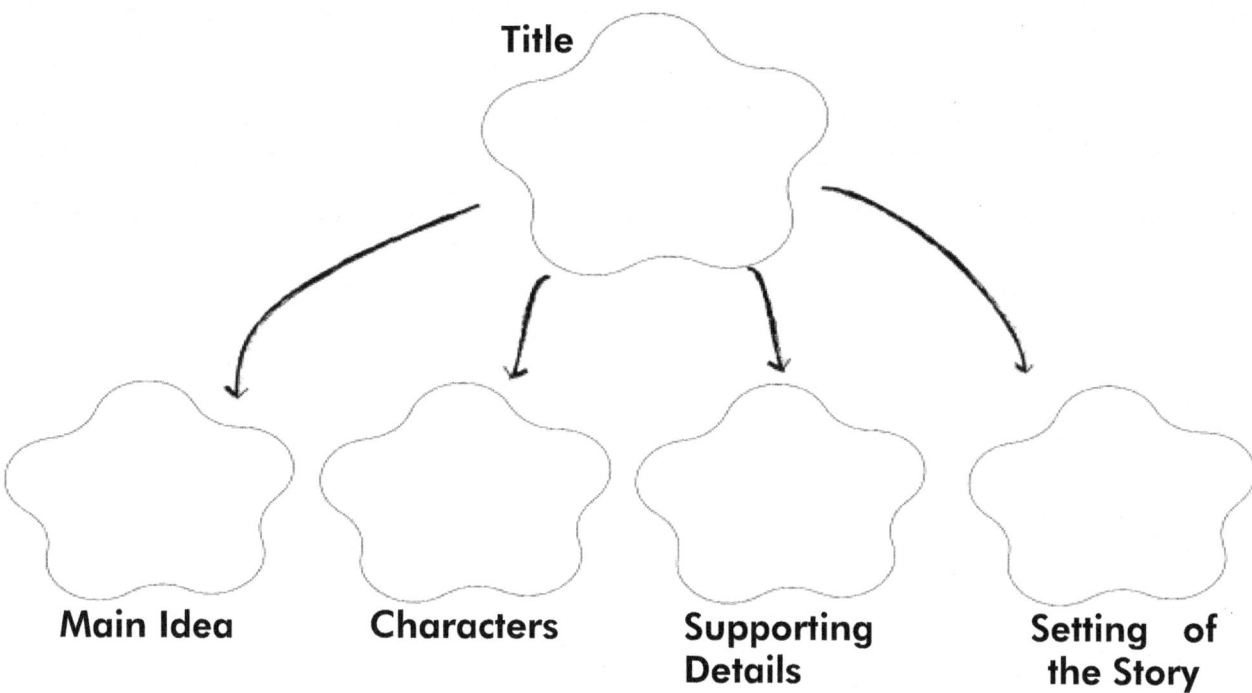

1. What is the setting of this story?

   Ⓐ It takes place at Marrah's house.
   Ⓑ It takes place at Marrah's school.
   Ⓒ It takes place on Marrah's bus.
   Ⓓ It takes place in Marrah's backyard.

Name: _____ Date: _____

Once there was a severe drought. There was little water in Tony's well, and he didn't know what would happen to the fruit trees in his garden. Just then, he noticed three men looking intently at his house.

He was certain that the three strangers were planning to rob his house. He acted quickly. He shouted out to his son, "My son, due to the drought, money has become scarce. There are many thieves.

Let us protect our valuables, and put all of our jewels in a box and throw them into the well. They will be safe there." He quickly told his son to put some large stones in a box and throw them into the well.

After reading the story, enter the details in the map below. This will help you to answer the question with ease.

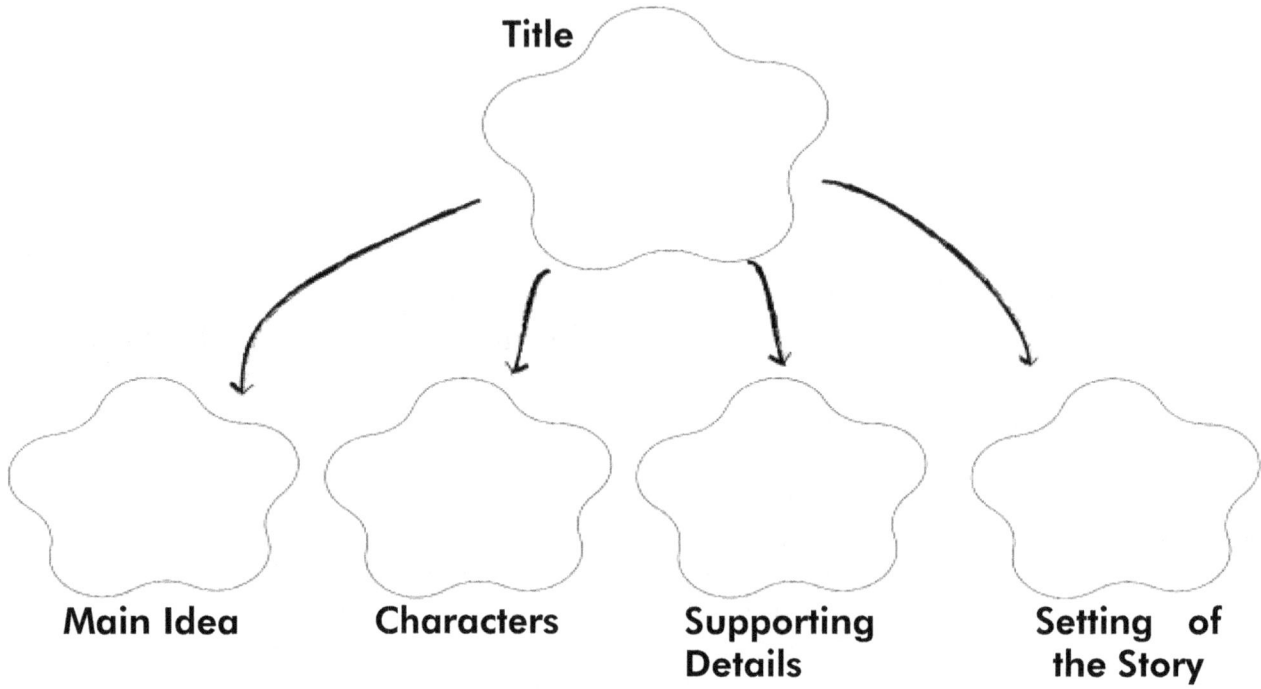

2. The author uses the phrase "a severe drought" to show that this story is set in a time when _____.

  Ⓐ there is too much rain.
  Ⓑ there is too much light.
  Ⓒ there is not enough light.
  Ⓓ there is not enough rain.

In the kitchen,
After the aimless
Chatter of the plates,
The murmur of the stoves,
The chuckles of the water pipes,
And the sharp exchanges
Of the knives, forks and spoons,
Comes the serious quiet
When the sink slowly clears its throat,
And you can hear the occasional rumble
Of the refrigerator's tummy
As it digests the cold.

3. What is the setting of this poem?

    Ⓐ It is set in a house.
    Ⓑ It is set in the stove.
    Ⓒ It is set in a restaurant.
    Ⓓ It is set in a kitchen.

RL.5.4 Figurative Language

1. This simile compares what two objects?

A cloud floats like a feather in the sky.

- Ⓐ It compares a cloud and the sky.
- Ⓑ It compares a cloud and a feather.
- Ⓒ It compares a feather and the sky.
- Ⓓ It compares the sky with nothing.

2. Which of the following is another appropriate simile?

- Ⓐ A cloud floats like a rock in the water.
- Ⓑ A cloud floats like a bird in the sky.
- Ⓒ A cloud floats like a leaf in the wind.
- Ⓓ A cloud floats like a cotton ball in a jar.

My daddy is a tiger
My mother is a bear
My sister is a pest
Who messes with my hair

3. What would be another similar metaphor for the author's sister?

- Ⓐ My sister is a bug.
- Ⓑ My sister is like a pest.
- Ⓒ My sister is annoying.
- Ⓓ My sister is like a bug.

Name: _____ Date: _____

RL.5.5 Structure of Text

1. When you read a humorous piece of writing, you usually _____.

    Ⓐ cry
    Ⓑ become serious
    Ⓒ write down information
    Ⓓ laugh

2. A passage that is an example of descriptive writing _____.

    Ⓐ is a letter written to a person
    Ⓑ creates a clear and vivid picture of a person, place, or thing
    Ⓒ describes an experience in a personal voice
    Ⓓ is a dialogue between two people

3. In a poem, we often find _____.

    Ⓐ rhyming words
    Ⓑ rhythmic writing
    Ⓒ dialogues
    Ⓓ 'a' and 'b'

4. Which of the following is not a genre of fiction?

    Ⓐ poetry
    Ⓑ mystery
    Ⓒ fairy tale
    Ⓓ informational

Name: _____   Date: _____

RL.5.6 Styles of Narration

1. Which sentence is written in first person point of view?

   Ⓐ Kelsey walked to school today.
   Ⓑ She walked to school today.
   Ⓒ I walked to school today.
   Ⓓ The neighbor walks to school every day.

2. Which sentence is written in third person point of view?

   Ⓐ I just won the race!
   Ⓑ Did you think the race was really long?
   Ⓒ She won the race.
   Ⓓ none of the above

3. Why is it important for the author to keep the same point of view throughout the whole text?

   Ⓐ It makes writing the story easy.
   Ⓑ It makes the characters fun.
   Ⓒ It makes the reader think about the message of the story.
   Ⓓ It keeps the story clear and easier to understand.

RL.5.7 Visual Elements

1. **How does a timeline enhance text as a visual element?**

    Ⓐ It provides factual information.
    Ⓑ It provides the key events mentioned in the text in the order that they occurred.
    Ⓒ It provides illustrations.
    Ⓓ It provides location information of places mentioned in the text.

2. **Please select the phrase that best completes the below sentence.**

The above illustration is titled "The Nutcracker".

Without looking at the image in detail, the reader might assume from only reading the title, that the image is about _____.

    Ⓐ the song "The Nutcracker"
    Ⓑ the commercial "The Nutcracker"
    Ⓒ the ballet "The Nutcracker"
    Ⓓ the star "The Nutcracker"

3. How does a map enhance text as a visual element?

Ⓐ It provides factual information.
Ⓑ It provides the key events mentioned in the text in the order that they occurred.
Ⓒ It provides key information as illustrations.
Ⓓ It provides the location information of places mentioned in the text.

RL.5.9 Compare and Contrast.

Number of library books borrowed in 2016	
Month	Number of books borrowed
September	660
October	670
November	570
December	475

1. From the above table, which two months had the largest number of library books borrowed?

    Ⓐ September and December
    Ⓑ September and October
    Ⓒ October and November
    Ⓓ October and December

2. Refer to the chart above to complete the sentence below.

    Students borrowed the least number of books in _____ 2016.

    Ⓐ November
    Ⓑ October
    Ⓒ September
    Ⓓ December

3. Pick the sentence that compares the above sets of words correctly.

    a. Math, Science, Social Studies, History
    b. Basketball, Soccer, Baseball, Tennis

    Ⓐ 'a' contains subjects related to cognitive activity whereas 'b' contains games that are related to physical activity
    Ⓑ 'a' contains subjects that we study whereas 'b' contains the games that we play
    Ⓒ 'a' contains subjects that are easy whereas 'b' contains games that are difficult to play
    Ⓓ both 'a' and 'b' are correct

Answer Key and Detailed Explanations

Reading: Literature

RL.5.1 Supporting Statements

Question No.	Answer	Detailed Explanations
1	C	There isn't any evidence in the passage that indicates that there was a storm that crashed the cupboard when the king was gone. The statement that people in the passage accidentally broke the glass cupboard is not accurate. However, it does say that the thieves broke into the palace and stole the glass cupboard. "None of the above" does not apply.
2	A	There is evidence in the passage that correctly supports the answer that the thieves took gold out of the cupboard. However, there isn't evidence that there was silver, diamonds, or stones taken from the cupboard, so these answer choices are incorrect.
3	D	There isn't evidence in the passage to support that the thieves were told to take everything out of the cupboard, to break the cupboard, or to take gold out of the cupboard. However, there is evidence to support that the thieves should have remembered to put something back into the cupboard each time that they took something out.

RL.5.1 Drawing Inferences

Question No.	Answer	Detailed Explanations
1	A	Choice A is correct. According to the first paragraph of the passage, it states directly that Sam was friendly. So, one can infer that he was helpful because he wanted to feed the weary traveler. However, there isn't any evidence from the passage to support that Sam was dangerous and cruel, or miserly and cunning. The last answer is partially correct, because Sam was friendly, but he was not miserable. Remember that if one part of the answer is wrong, then the whole answer is wrong.
2	D	Choice D is correct. In the passage, the reader can infer that Sam's wife likes food a lot, because can't resist it and loves to eat while cooking. One can also infer that the wife is cunning and clever, because she figures out a way to avoid telling the truth which is that she and her son ate the chicken.
3	A	The evidence shows that this passage is about being determined. The narrator did not give up. She listens to friends and takes a deep breath, but these are the details in the story, not the main idea. Remember that the sum of the details is the main idea which is what the story is mostly about.

Name: _____   Date: _____

Question No	Answer	Detailed Explanation
4	D	Choice D is correct. The evidence in this story that supports that Katie was nervous at the beginning is her blushing and wringing her hands. There is not enough information in the story to support that Katie was depressed. Do not confuse the crowd's excitement to mean that Katie felt the same way. While at the beginning she was nervous, she seems relieved at the end or glad that it was over. Because Katie had so many people happy for her, one might assume that she was friendly, but there isn't any evidence to support that in the story.

RL.5.2 Theme

Question No.	Answer	Detailed Explanations
1	C	The evidence clearly suggests that the purpose of this story is to show how giving back something in return for something else pays off. There isn't any evidence that shows the reader how to break the glass cupboard, or that this story was about the king. Although the king was mentioned in the story, he is not the main part of the story. Also, it can't be about the importance of gold, because there aren't any details to support its significance.
2	A	The last stanza of this poem states that one who has everything, but doesn't have time to stop and stare (look longingly at something), has a poor life. Another way of looking at this is to ask what good is it to have everything if you can't enjoy it? There isn't any evidence to support that life is good, so the other two statements are incorrect. Remember that if a statement is supported by a comma, both parts of the statement must be correct. If one part is false, the entire statement is false.
3	C	From the given choices, the best title for this poem is "Stop and Stare," because it supports the overall meaning of the story which tells the reader that a full life includes having time to stop and stare or just to rest and look at something for a while. "Life" is too general because the focus is not on life, but taking time to enjoy something in life. "Stare" and "Life and Stare" do not have supporting evidence in the story. The title can give the reader a clue to the message or theme of a piece, and "Stop and Stare" provides that information.

Name: _____ Date: _____

RL.5.2 Characters

Question No.	Answer	Detailed Explanations
1	B	In the first two paragraphs, the evidence clearly supports Katie and her mother as the main characters. They are key to the plot of the story. The story is mainly about Katie getting ready to perform and her mother's assistance. Katie's parents and friends are minor characters and were present to watch her perform, but they were not the focus of the story.
2	C	Katie's father and her friends, who were in the audience watching Katie's performance, are the secondary or minor characters in this story. The plot is not created around these secondary characters because they do not move the plot along.
3	A	The evidence in this story shows that Katie's mother is very supportive, because she had helped her to get ready the night before her singing performance. There is no evidence to show that Katie's mother was not supportive or that she didn't like Katie's singing. In the story, there is no evidence that Katie's mother wanted her to make friends, even though some of Katie's friends were in the audience. We cannot assume anything unless there is supporting evidence in the story.

RL.5.2 Summarizing Texts

Question No.	Answer	Detailed Explanations
1	C	This poem is about the importance of taking time to do things that you like. Even though the author does not directly state this, there is evidence to support this, such as no time to stop and stare. The author continues to list different things that the readers may have time to do if their life is too busy. The other answer choices are not as precise as the correct one. Remember to choose the best answer or the one that is the most accurate and complete.
2	B	Daniel was encouraged by his dad to try again. He finally tried and succeeded. The answers A, C, D are not found in the story. Answer B is correct.
3	B	It states that Daniel goes surfing with his dad. By reading the paragraph, one notes that they are enjoying getting ready and going. Only answer B is correct.
4	C	The second paragraph shows all of the things Daniel does to get ready early. Answer C is correct.

Name: _____   Date: _____

RL.5.3 Events

Question No.	Answer	Detailed Explanations
1	C	The saddle blanket is put on first, as noted in the passage. Answer C states that.
2	D	Each answer has details, but the correct order is D. This answer shows exactly how to saddle up a horse-blanket, saddle, tighten girth, bit and bridle after removing halter. The other details will not work with a blank after saddle, or tightening the girth before placing it on the horse.
3	B	Answer choice B has the correct order of sentences. Which demonstrates the order that Emily prepared, cooked, and ate her brownies? Answer choices A, C, D are incorrect.

RL.5.3 Setting

Question No.	Answer	Detailed Explanations
1	A	The setting of this story is in Marrah's house. Evidence of this is that she runs upstairs and downstairs, looks through mounds of clothes in her bedroom, and misses the bus, so her Mom has to take her to school. She missed the bus, and there was no mention of the backyard. Marrah's mother dropped her off at school, but there is no evidence of any action that takes place at school..
2	D	A severe drought means there is a lack of rain. Evidence in the story to support this is that the fruit trees in the garden needed water, and it just so happened that the trick that Tony played on the thieves provided some much needed water from the well that was able to water the fruit trees. The definition of a drought contrasts with the concept of too much rain. Also, there is no mention of there being too much or too little light.
3	D	The setting of this poem is in the kitchen because there is evidence of noise from kitchen utensils and appliances. The house is too broad and general, whereas the kitchen is more specific. There is no mention of a restaurant. The stove is in the kitchen and is does murmur but it is not the setting.

RL.5.4 Figurative Language

Question No.	Answer	Detailed Explanations
1	B	This simile compares a cloud to a feather using the word "like." The feather is located "in the sky." Choice A and D are incorrect because they do not apply to the definition of a simile.
2	C	Choice C is the best choice because it correctly uses the word "like" in the comparison of two unlike things, a cloud and a leaf. Just like a cloud floats across the sky, so does a leaf when the wind blows. In choice A, comparing a cloud to a "rock in the water" is incorrect, because a rock doesn't float like a cloud. It sinks in the water. In choice B, a comparison of a cloud to a bird is incorrect, because a bird doesn't float in the sky, it flies or glides. Choice D is incorrect because a cotton ball doesn't float. Be very careful that the first and second things have something in common.
3	A	My sister is a bug is a similar metaphor to my sister is a pest, because both comparisons indicate that the sister is annoying. A bug is a type of pest. Choices B, and D, are similes. In choice C, there isn't comparison being made. It is just a descriptive sentence.

RL.5.5 Structures of Text

Question No.	Answer	Detailed Explanations
1	D	When you read a humorous piece of writing, you laugh. You would not generally cry (unless you were just laughing so hard that tears welled up in your eyes), or take things seriously, because the laughter may be because of a joke. You would not write down notes during laughter unless of course you are writing down something that was so funny that it made a large audience laugh, and you just wanted to remember what it was.
2	B	Descriptive passages are created to present clear, vivid pictures of a person, place, or thing. Descriptive writing may not be the intent of one writing a letter, an experience in personal voice, or a dialogue between two people.
3	D	Choice D is correct. In a poem we often find rhyming words and rhythmic writing.
4	D	Informational text is not considered a fictional genre. However, poetry, mystery, and fairytales are appropriate fictional genres which might easily adapt to informational text.

RL.5.6 Styles of Narration

Question No.	Answer	Detailed Explanations
1	C	The use of "I" in the sentence shows first person, where the narrator is speaking about themselves. The use of Kelsey, she, and the neighbor show the third person point of view.
2	C	The use of she in the sentence is third person point of view. Choice A is first person. Choice B is second person.
3	D	Maintaining the same point of view throughout a story helps to keep the story clear and is easier for the reader to follow and to understand. The theme helps the reader to think about the message of the story. Descriptive words, well-developed character, and a great plot help make the characters fun.

RL.5.7 Visual Elements

Question No.	Answer	Detailed Explanations
1	B	When a timeline is inserted in the text, it shows the key events in chronological order as they occurred. A timeline should contain factual information. Also, a timeline is a type of illustration or visual element that may enhance text. A map, which is another type of illustration or visual element, is used to show the location of places.
2	C	After reading the title and without looking at the image in detail, a reader might assume, from prior knowledge, that the image is about the famous, classic ballet, "The Nutcracker." The presence of lyrics would suggest a song. A commercial may be an advertisement to sell or promote something. "The Nutcracker," as a star would likely be the focal point of the image.
3	D	As a visual element of text, a map provides location information of places mentioned in the text. A map may be considered a type of illustration that shows the factual information of things from the text, but option D is a more relevant answer because other illustrations can show factual information but only a map shows location.

Name: _____   Date: _____

RL.5.9 Compare and Contrast

Question No.	Answer	Detailed Explanations
1	B	According to the chart, the two months with the highest book check outs are September and October. The evidence in the chart shows that these two months are above 600 while the months of November and December are below 600.
2	D	According to the chart, students borrowed a total of 475 books during the month of December, which was the lowest number.
3	D	While sentence A describes subjects that require a mental activity, sentence B represents games that are played physically.

Reading Informational Text

Name: _____   Date: _____

RI.5.1 Inferences and Conclusions

1. Based on the sentence below, draw a conclusion about the way that Jan feels about the creature.

Jan took one look at the hideous creature and ran away as fast as she could.

- Ⓐ She thinks the creature is cute.
- Ⓑ She thinks the creature is scary.
- Ⓒ She feels sorry for the creature.
- Ⓓ None of the above

2. Select the phrase that best completes the sentence.

Kara's mother wakes up at 5:30 A.M. every morning so she'll have time to study for her college classes. This is the only time she has to study before she has to go to work. She takes college classes two nights a week. Every weekend, she volunteers at the local homeless shelter. She has been helping out there for the past three years.

From the information in the paragraph above, one can infer that Kara's mother is probably _____.

- Ⓐ married to a college professor
- Ⓑ a very hard-working woman
- Ⓒ tired of going to college
- Ⓓ None of the above

3. Select the phrase that best complete the sentence.

Victor took off his reading glasses and rubbed his eyes. He picked up his walking cane. Then he slowly used the cane to help himself up from the bench. Every day, it takes him a little bit longer to stand up. Every day, it becomes more difficult for him to walk.

From the information in the paragraph above, you can infer that Victor is _____.

- Ⓐ a young man
- Ⓑ happy
- Ⓒ an old man
- Ⓓ in good health

Name: _____   Date: _____

RI.5.2 Main Idea and Supporting Details

Salmon

A fish that is a great favorite with people is salmon. It begins its life in a small pool up a river. Far from the sea, the fish lays its eggs in a pool in the river. When the baby fish are a few inches long, they begin to swim down the river. As they grow bigger, they make their way towards the sea.

They jump over rocks, often with their tails first. Suddenly, they find themselves in the sea. The fish live in the sea for three years. They swim far away from land. How do they find their way back? These fish have a wonderful sense of smell. They remember the scent of their journey easily, because the river flowed to the sea and carried them there. After three years, most salmon swim toward the pools.

As soon as they reach a pool, the females lay their eggs. They lay their eggs near the edge of the water and cover them with sand. Soon the eggs hatch and the pool is full of small fish, getting ready for the long journey out to the sea.

After reading the story, enter the details in the map below. This will help you to answer the questions with ease.

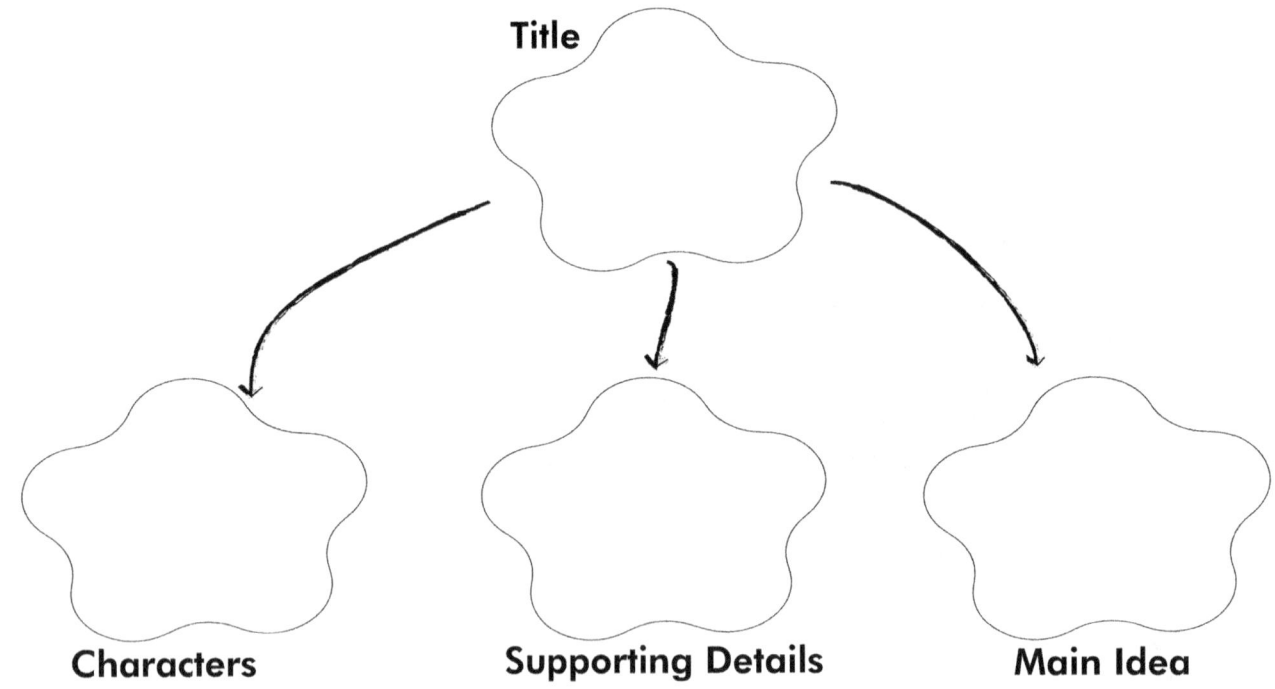

1. Which detail in the paragraph tells us that salmon jump backward over the rocks?

Ⓐ "When the baby fish are a few inches long, they begin to swim down the river."
Ⓑ "Suddenly, they find themselves in the sea."
Ⓒ "They swim far away from land."
Ⓓ "As they grow bigger, they make their way towards the sea. They jump over rocks, often with their tails first."

2. According to the passage, how long do salmon live in the sea?

Ⓐ six years
Ⓑ three years
Ⓒ one year
Ⓓ five years

Fruits begin to appear on the orange trees when they are three years old. Flowers and fruits may appear throughout the year. A very tasty and healthy kind of honey can be made from the orange flowers.

3. According to the text above, what is made out of orange flowers?

Ⓐ A tasty but unhealthy kind of honey
Ⓑ A tasty and healthy kind of honey
Ⓒ A bad tasting, but healthy kind of honey
Ⓓ Nothing is made out of the orange flowers.

RI.5.3 Text Relationships

Try Again

Surfing is one of Daniel's favorite pastimes! Every weekend when he has the time, he heads toward Port Aransas, Texas with his father. Daniel's family doesn't live far away, so it takes them only about 30 minutes to get there, if there is a short ferry line. They always make sure to get their things ready the night before. Daniel and his dad like to get an early start to their surfing day!

The night before, Daniel makes sure that his dad's truck is clean, especially the bed of the truck where he puts his surfboards. He also takes time to clean his wetsuit that he wears for protection and warmth. His mom usually makes sandwiches, and snacks ahead of time and puts them in the refrigerator to keep them fresh.

Daniel and his dad leave around 5:30 or 6:00 am when the sun is just coming up. Daniel has been surfing with his dad since he was very small. He remembers when his dad would ride with him on the surfboard.

When Daniel was about 9 years old, he fell off of a surfboard and hurt his leg and back. His dad rushed him to a nearby hospital for X-rays and a checkup. Luckily, there were no broken bones. However, the incident claimed Daniel so much that he refused to go surfing for several months. His dad kept encouraging him to give it a try. He told him, "If at once you don't succeed, try, and try again!" Daniel didn't want to try again. He was afraid of getting hurt and falling off of the surfboard.

Finally, Daniel went surfing with his father again. His father went out into the waves, and rode a wave in. Daniel went out on the waves, too. He stayed out for a long time without attempting to ride a wave back to shore. Daniel's dad began to wonder if his son had given up.

Just then a large wave began building up far out in the water. Daniel's dad was astonished! There was Daniel riding the huge wave all the way to shore without a problem. His dad motioned for Daniel to come where he was, but Daniel didn't. Instead he went right back into the water, and began riding wave after wave after wave!

It is amazing that fear can be overcome with one's personal best.

Name: _____   Date: _____

1. What happened to Daniel to make him not want to surf?

   Ⓐ His dad bought him a motorcycle.
   Ⓑ He was hurt in a car accident while going to the beach with his dad.
   Ⓒ Daniel was hurt while surfing and became afraid of trying again.
   Ⓓ None of the above

2. The reason that Daniel tried to surf again was because_____.

   Ⓐ His dad made him do it again.
   Ⓑ His dad encouraged him without belittling him.
   Ⓒ He was bullied into trying again.
   Ⓓ The weather changed so he could surf again.

The Traveler

A weary traveler stopped at Sam's house and asked him for shelter for the night. Sam was a friendly soul. He not only agreed to let the traveler stay for the night, he decided to treat his guest to some curried chicken. So he bought a couple of chickens from the market and gave them to his wife to cook. Then he went off to buy some fruit.

Now Sam's wife could not resist food. She had a habit of eating as she cooked. So, as she cooked the meat, she smelled the rich steam and could not help tasting a piece. It was tender and delicious, and she decided to have another piece. Soon there was only a tiny bit left. Her little son, Kevin, ran into the kitchen. She gave him that little piece.

Kevin found it so tasty that he begged his mother for more. But there was no more chicken left. The traveler, who had gone to have a wash, returned. The woman heard him coming and had to think of a plan quickly. She began to scold her son loudly: "Your father has taught you a shameful and disgusting habit. Stop it, I tell you!" The traveler was curious. "What habit has his father taught the child?" he asked. "Oh," said the woman, "Whenever a guest arrives, my husband cuts off their ears and roasts them for my son to eat."

The traveler was shocked. He picked up his shoes and fled.

"Why has our guest left in such a hurry?" asked Sam, when he came back.

"A fine guest indeed!" exclaimed his wife. "He snatched the chickens out of my pot and ran off with them!"

"The chickens!" exclaimed Sam. He ran after his guest, shouting. "Let me have one, at least; you may keep the other!" But his guest only ran faster!

Name: _____   Date: _____

3. Why did the traveler pick up his shoes and flee?

   Ⓐ He disliked Sam's wife very much.
   Ⓑ He thought Sam would be angry with him when he returned.
   Ⓒ Sam's wife tricked him into thinking her husband would cut off his ears.
   Ⓓ There were no chickens left to eat.

4. What happened as a result of Sam's wife's habit of eating as she cooked?

   Ⓐ Travelers stopped by for dinner often.
   Ⓑ Guests did not visit Sam and his wife's home.
   Ⓒ Sam's wife became very fat.
   Ⓓ There were no curried chickens left to eat.

RI.5.4 General Academic Vocabulary

1. What is onomatopoeia?

    Ⓐ A figure of speech where human characteristics are given to an animal or object
    Ⓑ A figure of speech where a word is used to describe a sound made by an object
    Ⓒ A figure of speech where a word or phrase means something different from what it says
    Ⓓ A figure of speech that draws a verbal picture by comparing two objects

2. What is an idiom?

    Ⓐ A figure of speech where human characteristics are given to an animal or object
    Ⓑ A figure of speech where a word is used to describe a sound made by an object
    Ⓒ A figure of speech where a word or phrase means something different from what it says
    Ⓓ A figure of speech that draws a verbal picture by comparing two objects

Oranges have many medicinal values. Oranges are the fruit with the greatest concentration of vitamin C. The skin of the orange helps to keep the fruit inside from becoming damaged and to remain clean. The thick, oily, and bitter skin does not allow any insects to get into an orange. Many kinds of useful oils can be <u>extracted</u> from the thick skin. Oranges are healthy and delicious.

3. What is the meaning of the underlined word?

    Ⓐ put in
    Ⓑ concentrate
    Ⓒ taken out
    Ⓓ placed

Name: _____ Date: _____

RI.5.5 Text Structure

Salmon

A fish that is a great favorite with people is salmon. It begins its life in a small pool up a river. Far from the sea, the fish lays its eggs in a pool in the river. When the baby fish are a few inches long, they begin to swim down the river. As they grow bigger, they make their way towards the sea.

They jump over rocks, often with their tails first. Suddenly, they find themselves in the sea. The fish live in the sea for three years. They swim far away from land. How do they find their way back? These fish have a wonderful sense of smell. They remember the scent of their journey easily, because the river flowed to the sea and carried them there. After three years, most salmon swim toward the pools.

As soon as they reach a pool, the females lay their eggs. They lay their eggs near the edge of the water and cover them with sand. Soon the eggs hatch and the pool is full of small fish, getting ready for the long journey out to the sea.

1. **What genre would the writing above be classified as?**

   Ⓐ A nonfiction passage
   Ⓑ Informative writing
   Ⓒ Realistic fiction
   Ⓓ Both A and B

2. **How is a Table of Contents helpful?**

   Ⓐ It organizes the text into manageable passages.
   Ⓑ It lets the reader know where specific topics or chapters are and on what page number they begin.
   Ⓒ It lists and defines some of the most difficult words in the text.
   Ⓓ It is a list of unusual words.

3. **Where is a Table of Contents located?**

   Ⓐ It is located at the beginning of the text.
   Ⓑ It is located at the end of the text.
   Ⓒ It is located in the middle of the text.
   Ⓓ It is located at the beginning of each chapter of the text.

RI.5.6 Point of View

I took one look at the hideous creature and ran away as fast as I could. I had never been so scared in my whole life!

1. Identify the point of view in the sentences above.

- Ⓐ first person
- Ⓑ second person
- Ⓒ third person
- Ⓓ none of the above

Kara's mother wakes up at 5:30 A.M. every morning so that she'll have time to study for her college classes. This is the only time that she has to study before she has to go to work. She takes college classes two nights a week. Every weekend, she volunteers at the local homeless shelter. She has been helping out there for the past three years.

2. Identify the point of view in the paragraph above.

- Ⓐ first person
- Ⓑ second person
- Ⓒ third person
- Ⓓ none of the above

Victor took off his reading glasses and rubbed his eyes. He picked up his walking cane. Then he slowly used the cane to help himself up from the bench. Every day, it takes him a little bit longer to stand up. Every day, it becomes more difficult for him to walk.

3. Identify the point of view in the paragraph above.

- Ⓐ first person
- Ⓑ second person
- Ⓒ third person
- Ⓓ none of the above

RI.5.7 Locating Answers

1. Where would you find the meaning of the word thespian?

    A) in an encyclopedia
    B) in a dictionary
    C) in a journal
    D) in an almanac

2. Where could you read the weather forecast for tomorrow?

    A) dictionary
    B) almanac
    C) newspaper
    D) encyclopedia

3. Where would you best look for a synonym for the word procrastinate?

    A) thesaurus
    B) atlas
    C) almanac
    D) dictionary

RI.5.8 Using Evidence to Support Claims

I went for a run this morning. Although I usually run in the evening, I decided to go in the morning because of the weather. It has been so hot this summer, so hot in fact, that I cannot run in the evening. Therefore, until we have cooler weather, I will continue to enjoy a morning run.

1. Which sentence indicates how long the author will continue to run in the morning time?

Ⓐ one
Ⓑ two
Ⓒ three
Ⓓ four

Sports can develop character. The players must abide by the rules of the game. Any departure from following these rules means foul play. Every foul stroke in a game involves a penalty. Therefore, players play a fair game. Fair play is a noble and moral quality.

Players become honest and punctual. The player develops the sportsman's spirit. Defeat does not dishearten a true sportsman. He does not feel over- excited if he wins a match. He learn to take both victory and defeat in stride. He never strikes an adversary.

2. Read the above paragraphs and identify the main idea.

Ⓐ Every foul stroke in a game involves a penalty.
Ⓑ Sports develop a player's character.
Ⓒ The players have to abide by the rules of the game.
Ⓓ Any departure from these rules means foul play.

My mother works extremely hard as a nurse. Each day she gives her all, and when she comes home she is dog tired. I like to help her take a load off, so I try and make dinner for her. I also clean the house and mow the yard outside. Today was even more difficult though. It rained like cats and dogs all afternoon, so I couldn't take care of the yard. Then, when I came inside to clean, I realized the kitchen sink was clogged and the washing machine seemed broken. I couldn't catch a break! By the time Mom came home, I had given up, called a plumber, and ordered a pizza. It's a good thing my mom always taught me that where there is a will, there is a way!

3. Which sentence explains why today was difficult?

Ⓐ two
Ⓑ four
Ⓒ six
Ⓓ eight

RI.5.9 Integrating Information

Suppose your parents asked you to attend your little sister's softball game.

1. Choose the sentence below that is written in a subjective point of view.

- Ⓐ The final score was 12 to 11.
- Ⓑ The game was really boring.
- Ⓒ My sister's team won the game.
- Ⓓ None of the above

Lost in the Woods

One day, a little girl named Tessa asked her mom if she could invite her friend Katelyn over for a sleepover. Her mom agreed. When Katelyn arrived at Tessa's house the next afternoon, the girls decided to go exploring in the woods close to Tessa's house. When the girls did not come back inside the house after a while, Tessa's mom decided to go looking for them. She walked to the edge of the woods and called out to them, but she heard no reply. After looking for them for about an hour, she decided to call 911.

Within hours, nearly 100 police officers and volunteers were searching for them in the woods. One of the officers brought Nickel, a search-and-rescue dog. Tessa's mom let the dog sniff one of Tessa's shirts so the dog could track the girl's scent. Nickel and her handler set off to look for the girls.

As they were walking down a trail, Nickel suddenly veered off the trail and headed downhill. Nickel led the volunteers down an embankment, and under a tree they found the two girls scared, but unhurt. In less than an hour, Tessa and Katelyn were back with their relieved families. The girls were thankful Nickel had found them. Nickel went home to wait for his next mission.

SAR Dogs

Search-and-rescue (SAR) dogs are special dogs with an acute sense of smell that are called in when a person is lost or trapped. SAR dogs search in remote areas and in places struck by natural disasters such as earthquakes, tornadoes, and hurricanes. SAR dogs are very effective and can often locate people when many volunteers can't.

Dogs make great searchers because of their powerful sense of smell. SAR dogs are trained to use their incredible sense of smell to search for people.

In 2010, SAR dogs from the United States found people trapped in the rubble after a devastating earthquake in Haiti. In 2012, SAR dogs helped locate people who were trapped in their homes after Hurricane Sandy hit the East Coast. These are only a few instances of when SAR dogs have helped people.

2. What is the purpose of the second passage "SAR Dogs?"

   Ⓐ To teach readers about earthquakes
   Ⓑ To provide readers with information about search-and-rescue dogs
   Ⓒ To give examples of types of search-and-rescue dogs
   Ⓓ To tell a story about a rescue effort

3. In "Lost in the Woods," what is the girls' attitude toward SAR dogs?

   Ⓐ They are scared of them.
   Ⓑ They are angry at them.
   Ⓒ They are thankful for them.
   Ⓓ They make them sad.

Name: _____ Date: _____

Answer Key and Detailed Explanations

Reading: Informational Text

Name: _____ Date: _____

RI.5.1 Inferences and Conclusions

Question No.	Answer	Detailed Explanations
1	B	Jan must have been scared of the creature. Choice A is incorrect, because the sentence said the creature was "hideous," not cute. Choice C is incorrect, because running away is not a reaction Jan would have if she actually felt sorry for the creature. Choice B "She thinks the creature is scary" is the best answer, because of the fact that the creature is "hideous" and Jan's reaction was to run away.
2	B	Choice B is correct. Choice A is incorrect, because the paragraph does not mention a husband. Choice C is incorrect, because the paragraph does not imply that Kara's mother is tired. Choice B is correct, because there is evidence in the paragraph that Kara's mother is hard-working such as the fact that she wakes up early to study, works at a job during the day, takes college classes at night, and volunteers on the weekends.
3	C	Victor is probably an old man, because he wears reading glasses, uses a cane to walk, and has trouble standing up and walking. Choice B is incorrect, because the paragraph does not state or imply that Victor is happy or unhappy. Choice D is incorrect, because the paragraph says that Victor has a difficult time standing and walking, meaning that he is not in good health.

RI.5.2 Main Idea and Supporting Details

Question No.	Answer	Detailed Explanations
1	D	The sentence "As they grow bigger, they make their way towards the sea, "and" They jump over the rocks, often with their tails first," is evidence that the salmon jump backwards over the rocks. If they didn't jump backwards, they would jump with their head first.
2	B	Sentence eight in the passage tells that live in the sea, for three years. Look for the evidence to support your choice in the passage, right down to the paragraph or sentence
3	B	According to the passage, a tasty, healthy kind of honey is made from the orange flowers. While this might be considered an opinion statement, it is the one that is used in the passage. However, there is no mention of other opinions stating whether the honey is bad or unhealthy.

RI.5.3 Text Relationships

Question No.	Answer	Detailed Explanations
1	C	Daniel stopped surfing after he was hurt while surfing. The passage is entirely about surfing, so Answers A, B, D would not apply.
2	B	The reason Daniel tried again was because his father encouraged him without making him feel badly. Answer B is correct.
3	C	The traveler grabbed his shoes and ran off, because he had overheard Sam's wife say that Sam would cut off the traveler's ears and feed them to the son. Choice A is incorrect, because the passage never gave the traveler's opinion about Sam's wife. Choice B is incorrect, because the traveler did not do anything to anger Sam. Choice D is incorrect. It is true that there were no chickens left to eat, but that is not the reason the traveler ran away. He did not know that weren't any chickens left.
4	D	Since Sam's wife had a habit of eating as she cooked, she ate all of the chickens that she had prepared. Therefore, there were no curried chickens left to eat. Choices A and B are incorrect, there was only one traveler or guest mentioned in the story. Choice C is incorrect. Sam's wife's appearance was not mentioned in the passage.

RI.5.4 General Academic Vocabulary

Question No.	Answer	Detailed Explanations
1	B	Onomatopoeia is the use of words to imitate sounds. Choice A is a personification which is the figure of speech that gives human characteristics to non-human objects. Choice C is an idiom, a figure of speech that is not meant to be literal because it means something different from what is stated. Choice D is a metaphor.
2	C	An idiom is a figure of speech where a literal meaning should not be taken, because the phrase means something different than what it says. A personification is the figure of speech that gives human characteristics to non-human objects. Words that imitate sounds are a type of figurative language called onomatopoeia.
3	C	The word extracted means to take out. The phrase "extracted from this thick skin" shows that something is being removed from the skin.

Name: _____   Date: _____

RI.5.5 Text Structure

Question No.	Answer	Detailed Explanations
1	D	Since the passage has factual information, it is considered to be a work of nonfiction. It provides information. Realistic fiction is a story that requires the use of characters and has a plot that is actually false but is based on real people, events, and places.
2	B	A table of contents will help the reader to see what chapters are in the book with the corresponding page number. If the reader is looking for specific information quickly, it is helpful. A glossary, located in the back of the book, will help define selected words found in the book. Headings are used to organize the text into more manageable passages.
3	A	A table of contents with each chapter in a book is located at the beginning of the text. The index and glossary are often found at the back of the text.

RI.5.6 Point of View

Question No.	Answer	Detailed Explanations
1	A	These sentences are written in the 1st person point of view. The author was the person in the story running away from the hideous creature. When the author used pronouns such as "I" or "me," one can tell that it is from the 1st person point of view.
2	C	The paragraph was written in the 3rd person point of view, because the author was not in the story. It was told from an observer's point of view. We know this, because the character (Kara's mother) is named. If it was told in the 1st person point of view, the pronoun I would be used. If it was told in the 2nd person point of view, it would use the pronoun "you."
3	C	The paragraph was written in the 3rd person point of view, because the author was not in the story. It was told from an observer's point of view. We know this, because the character (Victor) is named. If it was told in a 1st person point of view, the pronoun I would be used. If it was told in the 2nd person point of view, it would use the pronoun "you."

Name: _____   Date: _____

RI.5.7 Locating Answers

Question No.	Answer	Detailed Explanations
1	B	The dictionary primarily contains word meanings. To locate the meaning of thespian, you would use a dictionary.
2	C	The newspaper contains current events. If you are looking for the weather forecast for tomorrow or even for a one week period, the newspaper will have a meteorologist or weather reporter's predictions.
3	A	While you could use the dictionary to find a synonym for procrastinate, the easiest way to get several words that have the same meanings is to use a thesaurus. A thesaurus provides synonyms and antonyms of words.

RI.5.8 Using Evidence to Support Claims

Question No.	Answer	Detailed Explanations
1	D	The author states in the last sentence that until there is cooler weather, he will continue to run in the morning. If you look at sentences one, two, and three, you will not find evidence to support this.
2	B	The first sentence, the topic sentence or main idea, discusses the details about how sports develop character.
3	C	In the paragraph, following the sentence that said the day was difficult, is the sentence that tells why the day was difficult. The day was difficult, because it rained like cats and dogs.

RI.5.9 Integrating Information

Question No.	Answer	Detailed Explanations
1	B	Nonfiction texts are usually written in an objective point of view. A text written in an objective point of view is about an event, subject, person, or concept. It does not include the author's opinions, just facts.
2	B	The purpose of "SAR Dogs" is to provide readers with information about search-and-rescue dogs. Choice A is incorrect, because it does not teach readers anything about earthquakes. Choice C is incorrect, because examples of types of SAR dogs are not included in this passage. Choice D is incorrect, because it is not a story.
3	C	The first sentence in the last paragraph of "Lost in the Woods" reads that the girls are thankful for SAR dogs. There isn't any evidence in the passage to support Choices A, B, or D.

Language

L.5.1.A Prepositional Phrases

1. The object of a preposition is _____.

   Ⓐ the actual preposition
   Ⓑ the noun or pronoun that follows the preposition
   Ⓒ a word that identifies
   Ⓓ a word that shows direction

2. A prepositional phrase always _____.

   Ⓐ begins with a preposition
   Ⓑ ends with a preposition
   Ⓒ has a preposition in the middle
   Ⓓ none of the above

My mother plants orange trees in the backyard that give us wonderful fruit.

3. Identify the preposition in the above sentence.

   Ⓐ plants
   Ⓑ in
   Ⓒ backyard
   Ⓓ wonderful

L.5.1.B Verbs

Gerry and I <u>be</u> going fishing tomorrow to catch dinner for our family.

1. What is the correct way to write the underlined verb?

- Ⓐ been
- Ⓑ are
- Ⓒ am
- Ⓓ is

Last year, I <u>dance</u> a solo at my end of the year recital.

2. What is the correct way to write the underlined verb?

- Ⓐ dancing
- Ⓑ dances
- Ⓒ dance
- Ⓓ danced

3. In which sentence is the verb *make* used correctly?

- Ⓐ I make cupcakes right now.
- Ⓑ I usually make dinner for my family.
- Ⓒ My mother make homemade ice cream tonight.
- Ⓓ Billy make dinner for his family tonight.

L.5.1.C Subject-Verb Agreement

He _____ the chickens out of the yard and ran off with them!

1. Select the correct verb to complete the above sentence.

Ⓐ snatch
Ⓑ snatched
Ⓒ snatching
Ⓓ snatcher

2. The traveler, who had gone to wash his hands, _____.

Ⓐ returned
Ⓑ has returns
Ⓒ returning
Ⓓ return

The skateboarding show really _____ soon.

3. Identify the correct verb phrase from the above sentence.

Ⓐ be starting
Ⓑ started
Ⓒ should be starting
Ⓓ start

Name: _____ Date: _____

L.5.1.D Adjectives and adverbs

She is a <u>patient</u> teacher.

1. What part of speech is the underlined word in the sentence above?

   Ⓐ Noun
   Ⓑ Verb
   Ⓒ Adjective
   Ⓓ Adverb

This <u>exciting</u> movie is wonderful. The plot is quite <u>suspenseful</u>. Several parts are also very <u>funny</u>, and the <u>humor</u> adds much to the movie.

2. Which underlined word is NOT an adjective?

   Ⓐ exciting
   Ⓑ suspenseful
   Ⓒ several
   Ⓓ humor

My cousin used to be one of the _____ basketball players in the world. Now, there are only two players that are _____ than him.

3. Select the answer that has the correct adjectives in the correct order to complete the sentence.

   Ⓐ taller, tallest
   Ⓑ tallest, taller
   Ⓒ most tall, more tall
   Ⓓ tallest, more tall

L.5.1.E Correlative Conjunctions

_____ we go to the mountains for vacation _____ to the beach, I'll be happy.

1. Which set of conjunctions correctly completes the sentence?

Ⓐ Either, nor
Ⓑ Either, or
Ⓒ Neither, nor
Ⓓ Whether, or

_____ we can go for a walk in the park tomorrow afternoon, _____ we can go watch a ballgame instead.

2. Which set of conjunctions correctly completes the sentence?

Ⓐ Either, or
Ⓑ Either, nor
Ⓒ Neither, nor
Ⓓ Whether, or

I'm sorry, but I have _____ the money _____ the time to shop for new clothes right now.

3. Which set of conjunctions correctly completes the sentence?

Ⓐ either, or
Ⓑ either, whether
Ⓒ neither, nor
Ⓓ whether, or

L.5.2.A Capitalization

1. **Select the sentence that uses capital letters correctly.**

    Ⓐ A Person good at sports is usually given preference over others for admission to colleges.
    Ⓑ A person good at sports is usually given preference over others for admission to Colleges.
    Ⓒ a person good at sports is usually given preference over others for admission to colleges.
    Ⓓ A person good at sports is usually given preference over others for admission to colleges.

2. **Which of the following words or terms are capitalized correctly?**

    Ⓐ I, You, Texas, Katie
    Ⓑ I, you, Texas, Katie
    Ⓒ I, You, Texas, katie
    Ⓓ I, You, texas, Katie

3. **Which of the following words or terms are capitalized correctly?**

    Ⓐ Winter, Thanksgiving, Bobby, Cat
    Ⓑ Winter, Thanksgiving, bobby, cat
    Ⓒ winter, Thanksgiving, Bobby, cat
    Ⓓ Winter, Thanksgiving, Bobby, cat

L.5.2.A Punctuation

1. Which sentence has the correct punctuation?

   Ⓐ The boss entered the room and the workers became silent.
   Ⓑ The boss, entered the room, and the workers became silent?
   Ⓒ The boss entered the room, and the workers, became silent.
   Ⓓ The boss entered the room, and the workers became silent.

2. Which sentence has the correct punctuation?

   Ⓐ Please don't sing, until I have the webcam ready.
   Ⓑ Please don't sing until I have the webcam ready.
   Ⓒ Please, don't sing, until I have the webcam ready!
   Ⓓ Please, don't sing until I have the webcam ready?

3. Which sentence has the correct punctuation?

   Ⓐ Although the moon was out, the sky was dark.
   Ⓑ Although, the moon was out the sky was dark
   Ⓒ Although, the moon was out the sky was dark.
   Ⓓ Although, the moon was out, the sky was dark.

L.5.2.B Commas in Introductory Phrases

1. Which sentence uses a comma in the correct place?

Ⓐ By the way you left your book on the table, in the library.
Ⓑ By the way you left your book, on the table in the library.
Ⓒ By the way you, left your book on the table in the library.
Ⓓ By the way, you left your book on the table in the library.

2. Which sentence uses a comma in the correct place?

Ⓐ Every Christmas, my family travels to Vermont to visit my grandmother.
Ⓑ Every Christmas my family, travels to Vermont to visit my grandmother.
Ⓒ Every Christmas my family travels, to Vermont to visit my grandmother.
Ⓓ Every Christmas my family travels to Vermont, to visit my grandmother.

3. Which sentence uses a comma in the correct place?

Ⓐ After, we all were seated the speaker began his presentation.
Ⓑ After we all were seated, the speaker began his presentation.
Ⓒ After we all were seated the speaker began, his presentation.
Ⓓ After we all, were seated the speaker began his presentation.

L.5.2.C Using Commas

1. Which sentence uses a comma in the correct place?

   Ⓐ No I can't, babysit your little sister after school today.
   Ⓑ No I can't babysit, your little sister after school today.
   Ⓒ No I can't babysit your little sister, after school today.
   Ⓓ No, I can't babysit your little sister after school today.

2. Which sentence uses a comma in the correct place?

   Ⓐ The movie, starts at 7 o'clock right?
   Ⓑ The movie starts at, 7 o'clock, right?
   Ⓒ The movie starts at 7 o'clock, right?
   Ⓓ The movie starts at 7, o'clock right?

3. Which sentence uses a comma in the correct place?

   Ⓐ Kathy, will you drive me to the golf course?
   Ⓑ Kathy will you drive, me to the golf course?
   Ⓒ Kathy will you drive me, to the golf course?
   Ⓓ Kathy will you drive me to the golf, course?

L.5.2.D Writing Titles

_____ is one of the longest novels ever written.

1. Select a choice to complete the sentence above that displays the title correctly.

- Ⓐ *War and Peace*
- Ⓑ "War and Peace"
- Ⓒ War and Peace
- Ⓓ Both A and C

Has your little brother watched the movie _____?

2. Select a choice to complete the sentence above that displays the title correctly.

- Ⓐ *Bambi*
- Ⓑ "Bambi"
- Ⓒ Bambi
- Ⓓ Both A and C

My science teacher read us an article called _____ yesterday.

3. Select a choice to complete the sentence above that displays the title correctly.

- Ⓐ *Exploring Neutrons*
- Ⓑ "Exploring Neutrons"
- Ⓒ Exploring Neutrons
- Ⓓ None of the above

L.5.2.E Spelling

So as she cooked the meat, she smelled the rich steam and could not help tasteing a piece. It was tender and delicious, and she decided to have another piece.

1. Which word is spelled incorrectly?

    Ⓐ smelled
    Ⓑ tasteing
    Ⓒ tender
    Ⓓ delicious

Frantic now, Marrah lifted her sheets to look under them before droping to her knees in front of her bed. She pushed mounds of clothes out of the way as she continued to search for her backpack.

2. Which word is spelled incorrectly?

    Ⓐ frantic
    Ⓑ droping
    Ⓒ mounds
    Ⓓ continued

Katie stood before the crowd blushing and ringing her hands. She looked out and saw the room full of faces.

3. Which word is spelled incorrectly?

    Ⓐ blushing
    Ⓑ ringing
    Ⓒ looked
    Ⓓ saw

L.5.3.A Sentence Structure

My father warned us about the dangers of forest fires before he took us camping.

1. This is an example of _____.

- Ⓐ a simple sentence
- Ⓑ a compound sentence
- Ⓒ a complex sentence
- Ⓓ an incomplete sentence

My puppy always chews my slippers.

2. This is an example of _____.

- Ⓐ a simple sentence
- Ⓑ a compound sentence
- Ⓒ a complex sentence
- Ⓓ an incomplete sentence

The sleepy cat is.

3. This is an example of _____.

- Ⓐ a simple sentence
- Ⓑ a compound sentence
- Ⓒ a complex sentence
- Ⓓ an incomplete sentence

L.5.3.B Varieties of English

1. **Which sentence indicates use of dialect?**

   Ⓐ Would you like for me to help you paint the fence?
   Ⓑ Abe thought about it, but he changed his mind.
   Ⓒ I reckon I don't have time.
   Ⓓ That's ok with me.

"I appreciate you taking time out of your busy day to meet with me."

2. **What type of character would use this style of English?**

   Ⓐ a student speaking with a college professor
   Ⓑ two teenage boys watching a basketball game
   Ⓒ a patient talking to his doctor
   Ⓓ a woman talking to her best friend

"Yo, I'm psyched that we could do this today!"

3. **What type of character would use this style of English?**

   Ⓐ a student speaking with a college professor
   Ⓑ two teenage boys watching a basketball game
   Ⓒ a patient talking to his doctor
   Ⓓ a woman talking to her best friend

L.5.4.A Context Clues

Emily's mother <u>sternly</u> told her to finish practicing the piano, because she had taken long enough.

1. Select the best definition for the underlined word based on the context clues.

- Ⓐ happily
- Ⓑ beautifully
- Ⓒ sadly
- Ⓓ strictly

Her mother called again, and she could hear the <u>impatience</u> in her voice downstairs.

2. Select the best definition for the underlined word based on the context clues.

- Ⓐ patience
- Ⓑ annoyance
- Ⓒ endurance
- Ⓓ persistence

He <u>snatched</u> the chickens out of the yard and ran off with them!

3. Select the best definition for the underlined word based on the context clues.

- Ⓐ stole
- Ⓑ gave
- Ⓒ smelled
- Ⓓ glowed

L.5.4.B Roots and Affixes

1. Which of the following words does not contain a suffix?

   Ⓐ lemonade
   Ⓑ resident
   Ⓒ dormitory
   Ⓓ liquidate

2. What is the prefix of the word retroactive?

   Ⓐ retro
   Ⓑ ret
   Ⓒ re
   Ⓓ tive

3. What is the suffix of the word strengthen?

   Ⓐ then
   Ⓑ stre
   Ⓒ en
   Ⓓ st

Name: _____ Date: _____

L.5.4.C Reference Sources

tissue: a group of plant or animal cells that are similar in form and function

1. In which resource would you find this entry for the word "tissue?"

- Ⓐ a magazine
- Ⓑ a dictionary
- Ⓒ a thesaurus
- Ⓓ a glossary

abacus (n) Pronunciation: AB uh kuhss History: 14th century
an instrument made from beads and wires that is used to perform arithmetic

2. What resource is this reference from?

- Ⓐ a dictionary
- Ⓑ a glossary
- Ⓒ a thesaurus
- Ⓓ a math textbook

kindle: to start (a fire) burning

3. In what source would you find this text?

- Ⓐ a pamphlet about camping
- Ⓑ a thesaurus
- Ⓒ a glossary
- Ⓓ a dictionary

L.5.5.A Interpreting Figurative Language

1. **What is the meaning of the simile below?**

Without my glasses, I'm as blind as a bat.

- Ⓐ The person lives in a cave.
- Ⓑ The person is black like a bat.
- Ⓒ The person is blind.
- Ⓓ The person can't see very well without his or her eyeglasses.

2. **What is the meaning of the simile below?**

My teacher was as mad as an old wet hen when three kids didn't do their homework.

- Ⓐ The teacher lived on a farm.
- Ⓑ The teacher was crazy.
- Ⓒ The teacher was very angry.
- Ⓓ The teacher didn't assign any homework.

3. **What is the meaning of the metaphor below?**

Nick is a pig when he eats.

- Ⓐ Nick eats on the ground.
- Ⓑ Nick eats a lot, and he is messy.
- Ⓒ Nick is very fat.
- Ⓓ Nick makes pig-like sounds when he eats.

L.5.5.B Idioms, Adages, and Proverbs

She is really rubbing me the wrong way.

1. The above sentence is an example of _____.

- Ⓐ an idiom
- Ⓑ a proverb
- Ⓒ an adage
- Ⓓ a simile

Mrs. Smith's class is going bananas!

2. The above sentence is an example of _____.

- Ⓐ an idiom
- Ⓑ an adage
- Ⓒ a proverb
- Ⓓ a simile

A friend in need is a friend indeed.

3. The above sentence is an example of _____.

- Ⓐ an idiom
- Ⓑ an adage
- Ⓒ a proverb
- Ⓓ a simile

L.5.5.C Synonyms and Antonyms

1. Choose the set of words that are antonyms of one another.

    Ⓐ return, march
    Ⓑ alive, dead
    Ⓒ opened, broke
    Ⓓ collect, take

Once there was a severe drought; there was little water in Tony's well, and he didn't know what would happen to the fruit trees in his garden. Just then, he noticed three men looking intently at his house. He was certain that the three were planning to rob his house.

2. What is a synonym for the word rob as it is used in the above paragraph?

    Ⓐ cheat
    Ⓑ thieves
    Ⓒ steal
    Ⓓ borrow

3. What is a synonym for the word intently as it is used in the paragraph?

    Ⓐ lightly
    Ⓑ watchfully
    Ⓒ attentively
    Ⓓ both B and C

Name: _____ Date: _____

L.5.6 Vocabulary

1. Choose the definition of the underlined word in the sentence below.

My uncle plans to <u>retire</u> from the steel factory when he turns sixty-five years old in October.

- Ⓐ hide or conceal
- Ⓑ work additional hours
- Ⓒ clean up an area
- Ⓓ leave one's job and stop working

2. Choose the definition of the underlined word in the sentence below.

My favorite Greek <u>myth</u> is the story about Pandora's Box.

- Ⓐ a box to keep special belongings
- Ⓑ a family heirloom
- Ⓒ a traditional story
- Ⓓ a writing assignment

3. Choose the word that correctly completes the sentence below.

The people of the village were tired of being treated badly, so they made the decision to _____ the king.

- Ⓐ budge
- Ⓑ convert
- Ⓒ revert
- Ⓓ overthrow

Answer Key and Detailed Explanations

Language

L.5.1.A Prepositional Phrases

Question No.	Answer	Detailed Explanations
1	B	The object of a preposition is the noun or pronoun that follows the preposition. Generally, any word/words that are between the preposition and object of the preposition are adjectives.
2	A	A prepositional phrase begins with a preposition and always ends with a noun or pronoun.
3	B	The word "in" is the preposition that begins the prepositional phrase, in the backyard. Plants and backyard are nouns. Wonderful is an adjective.

L.5.1.B Verbs

Question No.	Answer	Detailed Explanations
1	B	Gerry and I are going fishing tomorrow to catch dinner for our family. Remember that the word "be" is not used alone as a verb. "Be" may be used as a helping verb with a main verb or a form of "be" such as is, am, are, was, and were.
2	D	Last year (indicates past), I danced a solo at my end of the year recital.
3	B	I usually make dinner for my family. Choice A requires the helping verb "am" making. Choice C requires the helping verb "is" or "was", making. Choice D requires the past tense, made.

L.5.1.C Subject-Verb Agreement

Question No.	Answer	Detailed Explanations
1	B	The verb tense has to agree with the subject, the verb "snatched" is correct. There is a compound verb in this sentence. The other verb, "ran," is in past tense, so both verbs must be in past tense. Adding "ed" to the end of the present tense "snatch" makes it past tense. Snatcher is not a verb. The "er" makes it a noun.
2	A	Traveler is the singular subject and requires a singular verb. Returned (past tense) agrees with the subject. If you read each of the choices in the sentence, the others do not fit because they do not agree in tense or number.
3	C	The adverb "soon" is a future time, so the verb has to be in the future tense. The phrase should be starting (soon) is correct. Choice B is past tense, and choices A and D are the wrong tense.

Name: _____   Date: _____

L.5.1.D Adjectives and Adverbs

Question No.	Answer	Detailed Explanations
1	C	Patient as it's used in the sentence is an adjective that describes the teacher. It tells what kind of teacher she is. Teacher is a noun.
2	D	Humor is a noun. Remember that words that follow "the" (which is an article and adjective), should be a noun, except for any adjectives that may precede the noun. Choices A, B, and C are adjectives.
3	B	Choice B, tallest and taller, is correct. Tallest is the superlative form of an adjective that is comparing more than two things, whereas the adjective taller, the comparative form, is used to compare only two things.

L.5.1.E Correlative Conjunctions

Question No.	Answer	Detailed Explanations
1	D	Whether we go to the mountains for vacation or to the beach, I'll be happy. Use the correlative conjunction "whether" in place of the word "if," and use the correlative conjunction "or" when you are expressing two different options.
2	A	When you're giving someone two options, use the correlative conjunctions "either" and "or." Answer D is incorrect, because using "whether" and "or" would form an incomplete or fragmented sentence.
3	C	I'm sorry, but I have neither the money nor the time to shop for new clothes right now. When you are expressing that two options are both negative, use the correlative conjunctions "neither" and "nor."

L.5.2.A Capitalization

Question No.	Answer	Detailed Explanations
1	D	The only word that should be capitalized is the first word of the sentence. People and college do not need to be capitalized because they are not specific names.
2	B	I is always capitalized unless it is used to spell a word that is not the first word of a sentence. Texas is the name of a state, and Katie is the name of a girl. However, you is a pronoun and should not be capitalized unless it is used as the first word of a sentence.
3	C	Winter, unless it's the first word of a sentence, should not be capitalized because it is not a specific name. Seasons are not capitalized. Thanksgiving, like all holidays, should be capitalized. Bobby is the name of a person, so it should be capitalized. However, cat is a common noun and isn't the specific name of a cat, so it should not be capitalized. Also, winter is capitalized if use as a proper noun.

L.5.2.A Punctuation

Question No.	Answer	Detailed Explanations
1	D	The comma and the conjunction "and" are used to separate the two sentences. Without the conjunction, the sentence would be a run-on.
2	B	This is a complex sentence because it has an independent clause (which can stand alone as a sentence) and a dependent clause, until I have the webcam ready, (which cannot stand alone as a sentence.)
3	A	The comma separates the dependent clause (on the left), from the independent clause (on the right). This is called a complex sentence. Therefore, it needs a comma to separate the clauses.

L.5.2.B Commas in Introductory Phrases

Question No.	Answer	Detailed Explanations
1	D	"By the way" is an introductory phrase. You should use a comma to separate the introductory phrase from the rest of the sentence.
2	A	"Every Christmas" is an introductory phrase. YUse a comma to separate the introductory phrase from the rest of the sentence.
3	B	"After we all were seated" is an introductory phrase. Use a comma to separate the introductory phrase from the rest of the sentence.

L.5.2.C Using Commas

Question No.	Answer	Detailed Explanations
1	D	No, I can't babysit your little sister after school today. Use a comma to set off "yes" and "no" from the rest of the sentence.
2	C	The movie starts at 7 o'clock, right? Use a comma to set off a tag question (right?) from the rest of the sentence.
3	A	Kathy, will you drive me to the golf course? Use a comma to set off a direct address (a person's name such as Kathy) from the rest of the sentence.

L.5.2.D Writing Titles

Question No.	Answer	Detailed Explanations
1	D	Choice D is correct. You can use underlining (Choice C) or italics (Choice A) to indicate titles of plays, books, newspapers, magazines, movies, and other complete works.
2	D	Choice D is correct. You can use underlining (Choice C) or italics (Choice A) to emphasize titles of plays, books, newspapers, magazines, movies, and other complete works.
3	B	Choice B is the correct answer. You should use quotation marks to indicate titles of poems, short stories, songs, and other short written works.

Name: _____ Date: _____

L.5.2.E Spelling

Question No.	Answer	Detailed Explanations
1	B	The correct spelling is tasting. The rule for adding -ing to the base word taste, which ends with an e, is to drop the e and add -ing.
2	B	The correct spelling is dropping. The general rule for adding -ing to the end of a word that ends with a consonant "p", preceded by a vowel "o", is to double the final consonant before adding -ing.
3	B	The correct spelling is wringing. If you read the context, the word that is required is a twisting and squeezing of the hands. You ring a bell, but you wring out your clothes if they are wet.

L.5.3.A Sentence Structure

Question No.	Answer	Detailed Explanations
1	C	This is an example of a complex sentence. "My father warned us about the dangers of forest fires" has a subject and a verb and is an independent clause. It can stand alone, because it has a subject and a verb and expresses a complete thought. However, "before he took us camping" has a subject and a verb, but it does not express a complete thought and cannot stand alone. Remember that a complex sentence has an independent and a dependent clause.
2	A	"My puppy always chews my slippers" is an example of a simple sentence that has a subject and a verb and expresses a complete thought.
3	D	The sleepy cat is. This is an incomplete sentence, because it does not express a complete thought even though it has a subject and a verb. The linking verb "is" should link the subject (cat) to something. To make the sentence complete, add an adjective like irritable after the verb "is" or a noun like Persian. The sleepy cat is irritable. The sleepy cat is Persian.

Name: _____   Date: _____

L.5.3.B Varieties of English

Question No.	Answer	Detailed Explanations
1	C	"I reckon" means "I think." This is an example of a dialect and it is often used in the southern region of the United States.
2	A	The sentence is respectful and formal. Also "your busy day" is another clue that a student could be talking to a college professor. Choices B and D are incorrect, because these are informal settings. Choice C is incorrect, because an appointment would be required to speak to a doctor. People use different styles of English for particular purposes and in different social settings. Different situations require different styles.
3	B	This is likely a statement said by a teenage boy to another teenage boy while watching a basketball game. "Yo" and "psyched" are informal terms used by young people in casual settings.

L.5.4.A Context Clues

Question No.	Answer	Detailed Explanations
1	D	The clue in the sentence is that sternly tells how mother spoke to Emily. Since she said that she had practiced long enough, it indicates that mother strictly meant what she said.
2	B	The clue in the sentence is that her mother called her again. Her mother is waiting downstairs for her to come down, and she seems to be taking longer than her mother expected since she called her a second time.
3	A	The clue in the sentence is that he took the chicken out of the yard and ran. The chicken was not given to him, which is why he ran. Taking without permission and running off is considered stealing.

L.5.4.B Roots and Affixes

Question No.	Answer	Detailed Explanations
1	B	The word resident, does not have a suffix. However, lemon - ade, dormit- ory, and liquid - ate, each have a suffix at the end.
2	A	The prefix retro- , is attached to the beginning of the word retroactive, meaning actively going back in time.
3	C	The suffix -en, is attached to the end of the word strength to form strengthen. The suffix -en makes strengthen mean to make stronger.

L.5.4.C Reference Sources

Question No.	Answer	Detailed Explanations
1	D	Glossaries give word meanings. A thesaurus provides a list of synonyms. A dictionary provides a lot of information (pronunciation, part of speech, definition), while a magazine doesn't typically offer any definitions.
2	A	A dictionary provides a word's part of speech, its pronunciation, its history, and its definition. A thesaurus, glossary, and a math textbook would not contain all of that information.
3	C	Glossaries give the meaning of a word. A thesaurus provides a list of synonyms. A dictionary offers many components of information (part of speech, pronunciation, definitions). A pamphlet would not likely offer any definitions at all.

L.5.5.A Interpreting Figurative Language

Question No.	Answer	Detailed Explanations
1	D	Without my glasses, I'm as blind as a bat means that the person can't see very well without eyeglasses. Bats live in the dark, and without glasses the person can't see very well, it's like they're in the dark.
2	C	The teacher was very angry, because three of the kids didn't do their homework. A hen gets mad when it gets wet. A teacher gets mad when kids don't do their homework. This is a simile, because it compares two unlike objects using like or as.
3	B	Nick is a pig when he eats means that Nick eats a lot and is messy when he eats. Pigs eat a lot, and they are messy because they're animals. When Nick eats, he probably gets food on his face and on the table. This is a metaphor, because it is a direct comparison of two unlike objects.

L.5.5.B Idioms, Adages, and Proverbs

Question No.	Answer	Detailed Explanations
1	A	It is not a literal interpretation, so the meaning has to be inferred. This idiom means that someone is getting on your nerves or they say or do something that one considers unkind.
2	A	The phrase "going bananas" generally means that there is a lot of excitement, chaos, or silliness.
3	B	A friend in need is a friend indeed has come to mean that if you help someone who is in need, they may be considered your friend or become your friend. They may be able to return a favor one day.

L.5.5.C Synonyms and Antonyms

Question No.	Answer	Detailed Explanations
1	B	Since antonyms are opposite in meaning. The words "alive" and "dead" are opposite in meaning. Choice D contains synonyms. Choice A and Choice B are neither antonyms nor synonyms.
2	C	The word cheat is not a synonym even though stealing could be considered a way of cheating someone. Remember that if you have two words that have some similarity in meaning, you should choose the best answer. Also, practice the words in the sentence to see if they read with the same meaning as the underlined word. Thieves rob or steal. If someone borrows something, it is assumed that they will return what they borrowed.
3	D	The word watchfully and attentively are both similar to the word intently. All three of these words are adverbs that describe the manner in which something is being viewed.

L.5.6 Vocabulary

Question No.	Answer	Detailed Explanations
1	D	The word retire means to leave one's job and stop working. People in the United States normally retire at the age of sixty-five when they are able to receive social security payments.
2	C	A myth is a traditional story usually about gods and goddesses of ancient Greece. Pandora's Box is a popular Greek myth.
3	D	The people of the village were tired of being treated badly, so they decided to overthrow the king. Overthrow means to remove from leadership.

Name: _____   Date: _____

Additional Information

What if I buy more than one Lumos Study Program?

Step 1 — **Visit the URL and login to your account.**
http://www.lumoslearning.com

Step 2 — Click on 'My tedBooks' under the "Account" tab. Place the Book Access Code and submit.

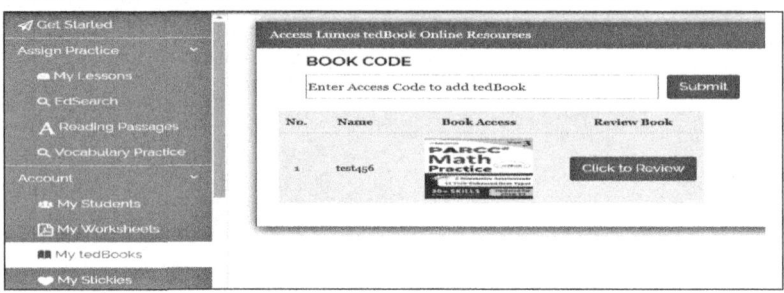

Step 3 — To add the new book for a registered student, choose the ○ Existing Student button and select the student and submit.

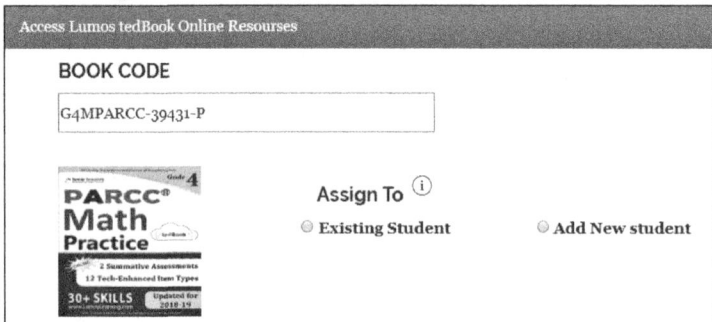

To add the new book for a new student, choose the ○ Add New student button and complete the student registration.

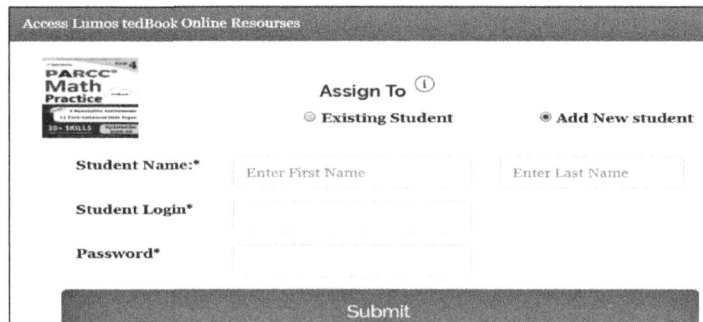

Lumos StepUp® Mobile App FAQ For Students

What is the Lumos StepUp® App?

It is a FREE application you can download onto your Android Smartphones, tablets, iPhones, and iPads.

What are the Benefits of the StepUp® App?

This mobile application gives convenient access to Practice Tests, Common Core State Standards, Online Workbooks, and learning resources through your Smartphone and tablet computers.

- Eleven Technology enhanced question types in both MATH and ELA
- Sample questions for Arithmetic drills
- Standard specific sample questions
- Instant access to the Common Core State Standards
- Jokes and cartoons to make learning fun!

Do I Need the StepUp® App to Access Online Workbooks?

No, you can access Lumos StepUp® Online Workbooks through a personal computer. The StepUp® app simply enhances your learning experience and allows you to conveniently access StepUp® Online Workbooks and additional resources through your smart phone or tablet.

How can I Download the App?

Visit **lumoslearning.com/a/stepup-app** using your Smartphone or tablet and follow the instructions to download the app.

QR Code
for Smartphone
Or Tablet Users

© Lumos Information Services 2019 | LumosLearning.com

Lumos StepUp® Mobile App FAQ For Parents and Teachers

What is the Lumos StepUp® App?

It is a free app that teachers can use to easily access real-time student activity information as well as assign learning resources to students. Parents can also use it to easily access school-related information such as homework assigned by teachers and PTA meetings. It can be downloaded onto smart phones and tablets from popular App Stores.

What are the Benefits of the Lumos StepUp® App?

It provides convenient access to

- Standards aligned learning resources for your students
- An easy to use Dashboard
- Student progress reports
- Active and inactive students in your classroom
- Professional development information
- Educational Blogs

How can I Download the App?

Visit **lumoslearning.com/a/stepup-app** using your Smartphone or tablet and follow the instructions to download the app.

QR Code for Smartphone Or Tablet Users

Other Books By Lumos Learning For Grade 6

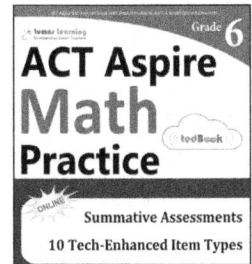 

ACT Aspire Math & ELA Practice Book

CMAS Math & ELA Practice Book

FSA Math & ELA Practice Book

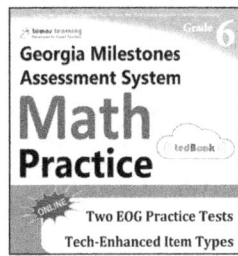 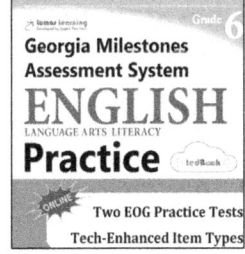

GMAS Math & ELA Practice Book

ILEARN Math & ELA Practice Book

LEAP Math & ELA Practice Book

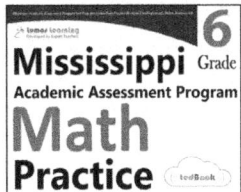 

MS MAAP Math & ELA Practice Book

MO MAP Math & ELA Practice Book

Other Books By Lumos Learning For Grade 6

MCAS Math & ELA Practice Book NYST Math & ELA Practice Book

OST Math & ELA Practice Book PARCC Math & ELA Practice Book

SBAC Math & ELA Practice Book

Available
- At Leading book stores
- www.lumoslearning.com/a/lumostedbooks

Made in the USA
Middletown, DE
15 August 2019